...iet of the animals
...s a bearing on the
...AL QUALITY, **and the**
...ss, of the food itself,
...EAT or MILK or EGGS.

...hael Pollan

"Nothing went unused...
it's incredib...
TO USE ALL THE ...
OF A PIG"
Naomi Pomeroy

...Emeril Lagasse

"RICH IN VIT...
AND HEAT-ST...
THIS TRADITIO...
IS A TOP-PICK...
FOR COOK...
AND NUTRIE...
Diane Sanfil...

"It's only polite
really if you knock
an animal on the
head to eat it all:
TRIPE, HEART, FEET,
EARS, HEAD, TAIL.
It's all
GOOD STUFF."
Fergus Henderson

"CHOLESTEROL LEVEL *and*
SATURATED FAT INTAKE
ARE NOT THE MAJOR RISK
FACTORS *for* HEART DISEASE."
Mark Sisson

"PRAISE
THE LARD!"
Stacy Toth

Everything
IN FOOD IS
SCIENCE.
The only
SUBJECTIVE
PART IS WHEN
YOU EAT IT.
Alton Brown

"DON'...
your gr...
WOUL...

You ma...
to you...
great-gr...
Mic...

"Go to the grocery store and buy BETTER
things. Buy QUALITY, buy ORGANIC,
buy NATURAL, go to THE FARMERS MARKET.
Immediately that's going to increase
the quality of the food you make."
Michael Symon

I always use my 'Holy ...
and bacon. My motto is, 'b...
I try to use bacon and po...

"Respecting and honoring
the pigness of
the pig is a foundation
for societal health."
Joel Salatin

I always use my
'Holy Trinity'
which is
SALT, OLIVE OIL
AND BACON

"*To me,*
LIFE WITHOUT VEAL STOCK,
PORK FAT, SAUSAGE,
ORGAN MEAT, DEMI-GLACE,
OR EVEN STINKY CHEESE
is a life not worth
living."
Anthony Bourdain

"DON'T EAT ANYTHING
your great grandmother
...

That is, the
of the animals
has a bearing
NUTRITIONAL ...
and the healthf...
of the food it...

BEYOND BACON

PALEO RECIPES THAT RESPECT THE WHOLE HOG

BY Stacy Toth AND Matthew McCarry

AUTHORS of EAT Like a DINOSAUR

FOOD PHOTOGRAPHY by Aimee Buxton

VICTORY BELT PUBLISHING INC.
Las Vegas

First Published in 2013 by Victory Belt Publishing

ISBN 13: 978-1-936608-23-2

Printed in the USA

RRD 01-13

*This book is
dedicated to Rina and Arthur Toth.
It is filled with their wisdom.*

Stacy's love of entertaining and her joy in sharing homemade food with others comes from her Italian grandmother Rina, who helped to raise her. Rina enjoyed nothing more than collecting and testing recipes and cookware. Much of the beautiful antique kitchenware featured in this book was hers. Sadly, Rina passed before we became authors, but she would have been overjoyed to know that *she is a part of this cookbook.*

Rina's husband Art was a man who brought a sense of tradition to his family; his Hungarian roots make paprika our family's favorite spice. Raised during the Great Depression, he taught his family to appreciate and *respect everything we are fortunate enough to have in our lives.* He loved organ meats; even at 95 years old, he was begging his family to find him blood sausage and head cheese. He inspired and taste-tested many of the recipes in this book before he passed, and for that we are grateful.

Our hearts and home are filled with the love of those who are still with us, as well as the memories of those who aren't, reminding us daily of the importance of human connection.

To our large family and those friends who have become like family to us, we cannot thank you enough. To each of you who are endlessly thoughtful, supportive and helpful, we are sincerely grateful and hope this book serves as a token of our appreciation.

TABLE OF CONTENTS

FOREWORD
BY JOEL

Joel Salatin is the third generation farmer behind the renowned Polyface Farm in Swoope, Virginia. The sustainable, natural farming practices he has implemented on his own farm have become the gold standard in the grass-fed, polyculture farming movement. Today, in addition to running his own business, he speaks around the world and has authored eight books on how he believes everyone should grow good, healthful food.

I'm a full time farmer in the pastured livestock business. As you can imagine, many of our customers are what I call "recovering vegetarians." The most common gateway to conversion occurs at the smell of bacon. We call it "the segue" for folks struggling to maintain the human abnormality known as vegetarianism.

On our farm, we love vegetarians because when they find out about the health and ecological benefits of pastured livestock, they go through a binge period to make up for lost time. As a farmer direct marketing our pastured pork to individuals and restaurants, I'm keenly aware that *a pig is more than bacon.* Many people don't realize that. In our fast food simple menu culture, few people think about the parts not posted on the #1, #2 options.

As farmers, though, we desperately need to sell the whole pig, from snout to tail, or we develop a mind-numbing and economically devastating inventory problem. On a hog carcass of 200 pounds, only about 25 pounds is belly muscle, commonly known as bacon. That means 175 pounds of non-bacon, or as Stacy and Matt suggest in this fantastic book—beyond bacon.

Perhaps the most valuable act that any eater can do to facilitate successful local food systems and vibrant pasture-based farms is to eat slightly blemished vegetables and fruit and to *eat all the parts of the animal.* Today's techno-sophistication offers the illusion that a simplified diet is acceptable. While ecologists preach diversity for healthy environments, too many Americans deny their own digestive flora and fauna the dietary diversity for optimum health.

Whenever I give a presentation about ecological integrity and local food systems, people ask: "What can I do?" This question has its ancillary issues regarding price, feeding the world, and culinary ignorance. All of these issues solve themselves when the answer to "What can I do?" is the simple

admonition: Do It Yourself (DIY). That common acronym, known far and wide, enjoys enough support in car maintenance, house maintenance, education, and psychiatry (know thyself) to keep countless talk shows, magazines, and blogs in business.

How about DIY food preparation, processing, and packaging? This brilliant book brings the DIY mantra to pork. In a day of profound culinary fear and ignorance, this book offers a DIY map for all who aspire to participate in the integrity food movement but are too afraid to start. The art and skill of healthy eating can be regained by marrying the ecologically sound farm to the delightful tastes and textures of delectable dining.

Lest she be slighted in this foreword, Aimee Buxton's food photographs excited my salivary glands. Indeed, *I could hardly keep the photos dry.*

One final thought: Stacy and Matt's healing journey began with a farm visit. Our farm, like all credible farms, does not have "No Trespassing" signs hanging at the farm entrance. We have an open door policy—full disclosure, open source. Call it what you will, but *Beyond Bacon* includes beyond pre-packaged, prepared, processed foods. It includes beyond typical vacation packages and entertainment venues. It includes visceral connections with food, starting at the farm. Come by anytime.

In that same spirit, Stacy and Matt open their kitchen, and share their expertise and journey. With this beautiful and straightforward manual, anyone can participate in the healing that is delightfully *Beyond Bacon.*

Joel Salatin
Polyface Farm

Rachel Salatin Photography

Before

PREFACE
BY STACY & MATT

Some three years back, we noticed that our family was pretty miserable. Like a lot of people, we didn't exercise, ate packaged and processed foods, and "cooked" with our microwave. We were a mess and so were our two sons.

On top of that, our family suffered from numerous health problems. While none were immediately life-threatening, they certainly led to a diminished quality of life and were likely signs of a diminished life span. Finian, our youngest, had recurring skin issues—red rashes on his face and eczema on his body. Our oldest, Cole, had asthma and ADHD symptoms. Matt had serious seasonal and pet allergies, depression, and ADHD. Stacy had an immune issue that elevated her white blood cell count. She suffered from depression, fatigue, and joint pain as well. We even had sleep disorders, high blood pressure, high cholesterol, and chronic heartburn. On top of everything else, the entire family was obese.

After the birth of our third son, we decided to make drastic changes. Instead of continuing down the destructive processed food path, we chose another: the Paleo lifestyle. This meant limiting our diet to *vegetables, fruits, nuts, eggs, healthy fats, and meats of the highest quality*, and eliminating all grains and dairy products. In addition, whenever possible, we eat fresh, organic, and locally grown foods.

Almost overnight our health improved. The change was dramatic and way beyond our wildest dreams. All of our health issues were resolved, we had renewed energy, we lost weight, and we felt stronger than ever. All told, we, the parents, lost more than 200 pounds, and our children crept back into normal height and weight ratios. We found that the better the quality of our food, the healthier we felt. We started buying fresh produce from farms and farmers' markets rather than grocery stores. We changed the way we bought meats and eggs, too.

WHICH BRINGS US TO THIS BOOK.

Which brings us to this book. When we started seeking out the best quality meats, we found farmers that employed remarkable and unique practices. We quickly learned that whether you call it grass-fed, grass-finished, humane, sustainable, pastured, free-range, or permaculture farming, the result is animals raised the way nature intended. And for us, that translated into the healthiest, safest, and most flavorful meat possible. Joel Salatin put it best:

"Respecting and honoring the pigness of the pig is a foundation for societal health." [1]

When we met our first pastured pig—so different from the heavy, confined pigs of conventional farming—we fell in love. A pig in its natural state is a beautiful animal, not the ugly, dirty thing most people think of. They are fascinating creatures, and arguably the most successful species of mammal outside of humans, serving as the perfect middle link in the food chain: sustaining the pinnacle links (tigers, wolves, humans) while actively regenerating the bottom links.

But we didn't just fall for their looks or their interesting place in the world. Let's be honest—pork tastes amazing! And pastured pork is even more rich and flavorful; because pigs are omnivores, their meat never tastes gamey. Then, of course, there's bacon, a food so perfect people have written books about it, made t-shirts extolling its virtues, created colognes and candles that smell like it—even a lip gloss that tastes like it!

You might say that we've gone whole hog for pork! Indeed, we now order and consume the entire animal. Yes, we love bacon as much as you probably do, but with this book we intend to teach you how to respect, appreciate, and eat *every* part of this truly special and delicious creature.

WHY WE WROTE THIS LOVE LETTER TO PORK

Pork is *delicious.* **That's probably not news to you. But bacon gets most of the love these days. Even in a world obsessed with food, we've forgotten how scrumptious a pork chop can be. But when you purchase a whole hog from your local pastured pork farmer, you quickly realize that there's only so much pork belly you can cure and turn into bacon. We discovered that there's a lot of exceptionally good meat left to cook and enjoy. With** *Beyond Bacon,* we hope to expand your horizons so that you, too, fall in love with the whole hog.

We realize not everyone's going to want to dive right into making Chitterling "Noodles" for Pho (page 116). And for the squeamish, we'd recommend not turning to the head cheese photos quite yet; it took us a while to warm up to even the *idea* of head cheese! But it didn't take long for us to see the benefits of incorporating organ meats, bone broth, and healthy fats from pastured pigs into our diet. Since adopting a Paleo diet, our family is more satiated, focused, and energized (more on that later). Our goal with *Beyond Bacon* is to remove your fear of organ meats and healthy fats, and provide delicious ways to incorporate these essential, nourishing, immune system-enhancing foods into your diet. Why not bolster your health as well as please your palate?

YES, WE SAID WHOLE HOG.

WHY THE FOCUS ON PASTURED PORK

Of all the pastured animals we could have devoted a cookbook to, *why pig?* There are two reasons. We found that when we priced out pastured and sustainably raised meats, pork cost the least per pound—less than chicken, beef, or lamb. That surprised us. Additionally, because pigs are omnivores, *their diet is naturally varied*, even when they are raised on a factory farm. This means that the *flavor of their meat* is enhanced, not changed, when they are fed the foods they would normally eat. This is not true of beef. In fact, when we serve pastured beef to friends, they often complain about the gamey taste and slightly tougher texture. No meat-eater, on the other hand, has ever rejected our pork.

We live in Virginia and have relatively easy access to one of the *best-known sustainable farms, Polyface Farms,* which is owned by the Salatin family. The Salatins have done a tremendous service in the area, consulting with other local farmers who are interested in converting to sustainable farming and the production of pasture-raised meat without sacrificing the economic viability of their business. Our family has visited several local farms in addition to Polyface, including *Mount Vernon Farm*—home to most of the pigs you see in this book, all photographed by photographer and farmer Molly Peterson—and *P.A. Bowen Farmstead, owned by Sally Fallon Morell.* What we've found is that humanely raised farm animals are docile, friendly creatures—and that goes double for pigs!

Sustainable farming provides more humane lives for livestock, which therefore produces healthier meat. It also benefits the earth beneath the animals' feet. On a sustainable farm, there are no waste pits full of toxins leaking into the soil, so they don't stink like the industrial farms you pass on the highway. And if they are managed properly, there are no problems with overgrazing, one of the causes of erosion. The result of this fantastic revolution is an abundance of farms working towards optimizing the environment, as well as the lives of the animals they are raising. And as we've gotten to know our local farmers, we've come to appreciate the varying flavors of the different breeds of heritage pigs.

Often what you'll find on pastured pig farms are old heritage breeds; some of them are very rare, and all of them look different. The amount of fat and muscle varies, and so does snout and jowl size. Colors range from white to black to brown to red to pink; some breeds are spotted, and others have a white band around the trunk that looks like a saddle.

Pig breeds are generally divided between those with longer torsos and greater muscle, which are bred for their meat (especially bacon), and those with a thicker fat layer, bred for their lard. The most common American breeds are the American Yorkshire (the pink ones you see in children's books), the whiter Landrace, the saddleback Hampshire, and the brownish-red Duroc. You'll also find hybrids. It is quite common to breed a red male, bred for its meat quality, with a pink female, bred for its mothering instincts.

Our friends at Mount Vernon Farm raise the Tamworth breed— sometimes referred to as "bacon pigs" because of their long belly and high muscle-to-fat content. These are the hogs that introduced us to pastured pork, and the breed used for the majority of the recipes in this book.

You just get more belly with a Tamworth, and who doesn't want that?

If you choose to cook with meat from a breed other than the Tamworth, with a different volume of meat or a higher or lower percentage of body fat, *you might need to adjust cooking times*. But the good news about cooking pork is that the meat is naturally fatty so many of the standard cuts baste themselves. As a result, unless you excessively trim the fat, you'll easily achieve a moist result.

Whatever breed you choose to cook with, however, know that freshly butchered, pastured meat will look nothing like what you buy in a grocery store. The appearance might startle you at first. Just remember that those rows and rows of pork chops in freezer cases are made in a factory, which is why they all look identical.

So why buy pastured pork? First and foremost, there are the ethical concerns. Industrial pig farming hurts the animal; it's a gruesome process that pays no mind to suffering. The second biggest reason is health—the pig's and yours.

Why wouldn't you want to *optimize the nutritional value of the meat you eat?* The best way to do that is to feed the animal a species-appropriate diet. If a pig is raised humanely, on food it would naturally eat, you can expect a greater proportion of healthy omega-3 fatty acids, plus micronutrients you'd never find in a conventionally raised pig.

It's important to note that *all pigs receive a supplemental diet beyond the food they graze on*, whether they graze in a pasture or the forest. Pigs on small farms often receive scraps left over from the farmer's food, and farmers who raise more than a few pigs supplement with feed. This can vary in quality and that's what you need to investigate before you purchase pork from a local farmer. We always ask about the ingredients in the feed, the quantity used, and if it has been genetically modified. Make the best choices you can, and know that if a pastured pig gets just a portion of its diet through supplemental, conscientiously-chosen corn or soy feed, it will never be as detrimental to your health as the meat from a hog raised on an industrial farm.

Best of all, you'll be consuming an animal that was healthy when it died. Pigs raised on industrial farms live in cramped, dirty conditions—environments that encourage disease. This is why they are pumped full of antibiotics when they are alive. Ask yourself: Do you want to bring home bacon from a drug-filled pig that was likely close to death before it was slaughtered?

"Animals that we eat are raised for food in the most economical way possible, and the serious food producers do it in the most humane way possible. I think anyone who is a carnivore needs to understand that meat does not originally come in these neat little packages."[2]

–Julia Child

HOW *TO* FIND & AFFORD PASTURED PORK

Whether you live on an isolated ranch somewhere or in a giant city, you can find a source for pastured pork. To begin, see if you can locate a humane farmer who lives relatively close to you. We live in a densely populated suburb, but we don't have to go too far to reach farmland. Our favorite lamb farm is an hour's drive away. Mount Vernon Farm is another hour further west, and Polyface is another hour beyond that. And all three deliver to our city regularly!

If a pair of East Coast suburbanites can find farms to visit and purchase from, you can too! The website EatWild.com has a giant directory of sustainable farms with pasture-raised animal farms, as well as interactive maps to help you find the ones closest to you. We definitely believe that you should *visit a local farm*. For us, it was *truly life changing*.

But what if you can't drive that far? What if you live in a city and don't own a car? Well, maybe your local farm can come to you! These days, many farmers sell directly to the consumer at designated drop locations. Contact your closest sustainable farm and see if they do something along these lines.

Even if there is no local farm delivering in your area, you may not be out of luck. Most densely populated areas have farmers' markets and co-ops where high quality pastured meat is sold. Contact your town or county office to determine if there's a market where you live; they will know since they issue the permits.

> "Go to the grocery store and buy better things. Buy quality, buy organic, buy natural, go to the farmers' market. Immediately that's going to increase the quality of the food you make."[3]
>
> **– Michael Symon, Iron Chef**

IF ALL ELSE FAILS, MAYBE YOU, TOO, HAVE A DON.

Don Roden owns The Organic Butcher of McLean, and he, like other local butchers, is accommodating, knowledgeable, and helpful. When you walk into his shop, you are blown away by the vast selection of humanely and sustainably raised meat—from duck to pork to antelope to wild boar! His shop also sources quality food, much like co-ops and local farm stores do.

Your butcher should be able to tell you the sources of all the meat he sells, including information about the farming techniques used. He should also be able to procure the more unusual cuts of pork used in this book. If you're going to have a hard time finding a head or a liver in your state because of local food laws, he'll know about that, too. We highly recommend hanging out with your butcher and asking general questions. Butchering is a fascinating art. We learned a ton from Don about the history of certain cuts of meat and their ideal preparation.

That said, *the most affordable way to purchase pastured pork is the old-fashioned way: Buy the entire animal from a local farm that you can trust.* In our area, a whole butchered pig costs between three and four dollars per pound, plus a separate fee per pound for the butchering. The total weight of the meat from a single whole pig can go as high as a couple hundred pounds, so that works out to an investment of several hundred dollars. That might sound like a lot, but it's well worth the expense.

We saw these fantastic prints by Drywell Art hanging in a farm shop, and bought a set for ourselves. We have studied the various cuts for years and still don't have it all straight. If you're feeling overwhelmed, just ask your farmer to recommend some options. You'll quickly learn what you like and what you might want to do differently next time. As we mentioned, your farmer or butcher can also help by reviewing a cut sheet, similar to the one on page 27. Don't get frustrated, take your time, have patience, and ask questions!

WHEN ORDERING A WHOLE ANIMAL, THERE ARE SEVERAL THINGS TO CONSIDER:

- **Where is your farmer taking the animals to be slaughtered and butchered?** Once you order your pig, the farmer will select an animal that has reached the appropriate age and weight to bring to slaughter. Most farms do not slaughter and butcher on site; they transport the live animal to a place that has the facilities and permits to do it. This is called processing, and how it is done will affect many things, including what organ meats you can attain, whether skin, bones and fat are available to you, and whether you can receive the head and feet. Since you are paying for this service, and the weight you are charged includes these parts, ask if the processor can provide you with all the parts selected.

- **What are your options for dividing up the meat?** Consider how you'd like your animal butchered. Your farmer will have a cut sheet (similar to the one on page 27) that will walk you through your order. You will need to decide, for example, whether you want ribs and backbone or bone-in rib chops, since you can't have both. Consider whether you want the shoulder cut into the large picnic and Boston butt cuts, or if you want smaller roasts. Do you want feet and tail? Do you want a whole head, or just the most desirable parts—the tongue and jowl—separated?

- **To share or not to share?** Going in on a pig with some friends will make it more affordable, but it also might lead to fights over the 8-16 pounds of bacon or belly per pig. The key is to find a very organized friend who knows their way in and around a spreadsheet and have people sign up for cuts at an agreed upon price per pound. The other option is to simply split the pig in half. Either way, since you don't know the final weight of the pig until it goes to processing, the cost is only approximate until you get the final invoice from your farmer. Make sure you trust whomever you share your pig with, and definitely ask them for a deposit, since your farm will require one!

- **Finally, you'll need to navigate a cut sheet.** This is the piece of paper that will list all the possible cut choices. You just tick off the appropriate boxes. You'll also need to decide how you want your cuts packaged. To help you understand what to expect, we've provided a sample on page 27.

WHAT QUESTIONS will YOU NEED to ANSWER when ordering a WHOLE PIG?

Beyond the normal cut sheets, you'll have to decide what organs you want. Always ask for the liver, tongue, and heart. They are *particularly nutritious*. Be sure to get the bones and fat as well. We recommend you ask for every part of the pig—from the glands (sweet breads) to the trotters. This book teaches you how to cook them all!

YOU'LL BE ASKED THE FOLLOWING QUESTIONS ON THE CUT SHEET:

- If you're getting chops, what thickness do you want, how many per pack, and do you want them bone-in or boneless?

- How big do you want your ground meat packages to be?

- What size do you want the roasts?

- Do you want any of your bones cut for marrow (long bones sliced down the center) or are meaty soup bones all you are after?

- Do you want the leaf fat separated from the back fat? (We separate them because the taste between leaf fat and back fat is different.)

- What do you want to do with the loin? Do you want loin chops (T-bone pork chops) or loin roasts (including the tenderloin)? Do you want rib chops (the pork chops with the bone on the side) or rib roasts?

- For the side pork (belly and spare ribs), do you want bacon (most butchers will process belly into bacon for you) or fresh belly? If you are ordering bacon, make sure it is thick cut and naturally cured.

- If you order food from your purveyor, such as bacon or sausage, make sure to read the ingredient list.

- Finally, you'll need to know the difference between butts, shoulders, and hams. In the pig world, Boston butt is the upper part of the shoulder and picnic is the lower part (the front legs). Ham is the cut that comes from the pig's behind, which is part of the back leg. How do you want it prepared? Do you want it whole, for example, because it's June and you have six months to cure a Christmas ham? Or perhaps they should cut it into roasts or 1 inch-thick bone-in steaks? They may offer to smoke it for you, or you can ask them to grind it all.

Some purveyors offer different options, like turning part or all of the ground meat into sausage. They may offer the backbone cut or other unusual cuts. Pay attention to all the options so you can get the most out of your pig.

26

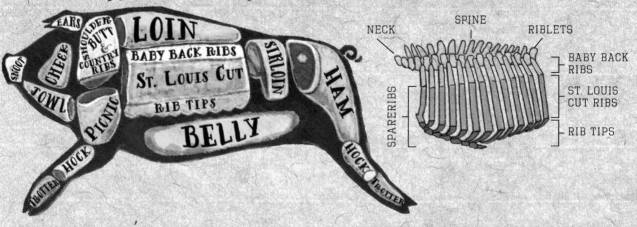

Hog Anatomy

LOIN
BABY BACK RIBS
St. Louis Cut
RIB TIPS
BELLY
SIRLOIN
HAM
EARS
SNOUT
CHEEK
JOWL
SHOULDER
BUTT & COUNTRY RIBS
PICNIC
HOCK
TROTTER
HOCK
TROTTER

Rib Cuts

NECK
SPINE
RIBLETS
BABY BACK RIBS
ST. LOUIS CUT RIBS
RIB TIPS
SPARERIBS

FRONT SHOULDER: ☐ Boneless ☐ Bone-in ☐ Smoked ☐ Fresh

BOSTON BUTT ROAST: ☐ Boneless ☐ Bone-in
OR
COUNTRY-STYLE RIBS: _____ Lbs per package

LOIN END ROAST OR PORK CHOPS: ☐ Boneless ☐ Bone-in
THICKNESS OF CHOPS: ☐ 3/4" ☐ 1" ☐ 1 1/4" ☐ 1 1/2"
_____ Chops per package

TENDERLOIN OR RIB CHOPS: ☐ Boneless ☐ Bone-in
THICKNESS OF CHOPS: ☐ 3/4" ☐ 1" ☐ 1 1/4" ☐ 1 1/2"
_____ Chops per package

HAM: ☐ Boneless ☐ Bone-in ☐ Smoked ☐ Fresh
CENTER SLICES (HAM STEAKS): ☐ 1/2" ☐ 1" ☐ 1 1/2"
☐ Whole _____ Slices per package

BELLY: ☐ Smoked bacon ☐ Fresh bacon ☐ Whole belly
_____ Lbs per package

SAUSAGE: ☐ Breakfast ☐ Kielbasa ☐ Hot Italian
☐ Andouille ☐ Sweet Italian ☐ Chorizo
☐ Links ☐ Patties _____ Lbs per package

HOCKS: ☐ Smoked ☐ Fresh

RIBS: ☐ Baby back ribs ☐ Spareribs ☐ St. Louis cut ribs ☐ Rib tips

---

WOULD YOU LIKE ANY OF THE FOLLOWING (CHECK ANY THAT YOU DO WANT)?
☐ Heart ☐ Liver
☐ Tongue ☐ Bones
☐ Trotters ☐ Kidneys

PACKAGING:
☐ Freezer wrap ☐ Cryovac

Forrest Pritchard,
Smith Meadow Farm in Berryville, Virginia,
Author of "Gaining Ground"

HISTORY *of* PIG CULTIVATION

Over roughly *10,000 years of selective breeding* (for size, speed of growth, demeanor, litter size, and fat-to-muscle ratio), man has molded these monsters into the delicious and cute heritage breeds you see today. Still, you only have to look at the wild, tusked boars that still roam the globe to see what made them so appealing to Neolithic man: They are supremely hearty and adaptable.

The original pigs spanned the globe, thriving in a variety of climates and living conditions—from Norway to North Africa to Japan. Pigs can subsist on extremely varied diets, from meat to grains, and those big bellies make them particularly adept at storing energy. Then, as now, they were completely satisfied by the food we routinely tossed out, which they then turned into dense and nutritious sources of food for humans. Even better, they are easy to preserve as dried, cured, or salted meats. Sows are extremely prolific, too, as each litter produces between 6 and 12 piglets. All of this made the original wild boars ideal for domestication.

Humans began to domesticate animals around 10,000 years ago. It's believed that sheep and goats were the first to be raised (rather than hunted) as a source of food. They were the standard animals of the nomadic pastoralists. Once Neolithic man began to settle down in one place—around 7,000 BC—oxen and *Sus scrofa*—wild pigs or boar—were domesticated.[5] These original pigs probably looked similar to the wild boars of today: grey or brown in color, around three feet tall and weighing 300 pounds, with large tusks. They are not the most dangerous animals to hunt—not even close—but they can be fearsome and inflict serious damage if you're not careful. *Stacy's father has frightened many a visitor with the mounted boar head on his wall.*

Much as we'd like to say that pigs are perfect, they are not. Their oddest flaw is their inability to cool themselves. They have fewer functional sweat glands than other mammals, which means temperature adjustment in hot climates is impossible. (The pink and white breeds have an additional problem; thanks to minimal fur and melanin, they routinely burn in the sun!) But being the adaptable creatures that they are, pigs have found natural forms of air conditioning, which is why you see them wallowing in mud pits or under shady trees. If they didn't do this, pigs would routinely die from heatstroke.

The downside to pig farming today, of course, is that the animals rarely roam and graze as they once did, and the way nature intended. Industrial commercial farming is now the norm. Everything about this system (called a Concentrated Animal Feeding Operation, or CAFO) is geared toward profit: bringing as many animals as possible to slaughter, at the cheapest price possible. *Little attention is paid to animal welfare, quality of meat, or negative impact on the environment.* Sows are kept in pens so tiny they can't move during pregnancy. Weaned piglets are crowded together in small stalls and fed only genetically modified grain-based feed. All the stalls are indoors, to prevent the risk of heat stroke. Pigs are preemptively altered to make them less aggressive. Teeth are blunted and tails are docked. Antibiotics are routinely injected since the cramped and dirty conditions encourage infection. Lagoons of pig feces leak into the ground water, polluting surrounding water sources.

If this seems like a terrible way to procure meat, consider that conditions now are better than they were twenty years ago, at least in terms of food safety. In the past, pigs were fed a meal containing the meat and bone of fellow pigs. Any pathologist will tell you that feeding raw meat and brains to animals is an excellent way to transmit disease into your meat. This is the cause of Trichinosis, a serious parasitic infection that occurs in raw or undercooked pork, and mad cow disease (Bovine Spongiform Encephalopathy—or Variant Creutzfeldt-Jakob Disease when it enters humans). In the mid-20th century, there were more than 500 cases of trichina infection per year in the United States. That has now dropped to under 12 per year, and those cases are usually due to wild game consumption.[6]

The tragedy of this system is obvious. With the focus on bringing pigs to slaughter in an efficient and profitable manner, the practice that produces the happiest animals and the healthiest meat was discarded. As Joel Salatin says, "it's better to allow the pigs to express their pigness. Healthy pigs fully engaged in pig living will produce your best pork."

What does being a pig mean, though? For starters, pigs have always roamed the woods and grasslands in small groups, foraging for a variety of food. They are true opportunistic omnivores—meaning that they will eat anything, from fruits and vegetables to small animals and carrion. Pigs love to dig and root in the ground and need to cool off in water and mud. They are also relatively smart (as all of us omnivores tend to be) and need activity to exercise their brains. Let them grow as piggy as they'd like and you'll be rewarded with superior pork products.

"That is, the diet of the animals we eat has a bearing on the nutritional quality, and the healthfulness, of the food itself, whether it is meat or milk or eggs."[7]

–Michael Pollan

THEY'RE HAPPY
Because they eat
LARD

Issued by the Lard Information Council

THE SCIENCE OF PORK AND SATURATED FAT

Before our family adopted the Paleo lifestyle, we fully believed in the idea that a diet high in saturated fat and cholesterol was the cause of heart disease (this is a scientific idea called the diet-heart hypothesis). Even after we began this lifestyle, we continued to think this way, since the first book we read was *The Paleo Diet* by Dr. Loren Cordain. At the time of the writing of that book, Cordain advocated a low fat approach due to heart disease concerns. Since then, the *importance of fat has spread throughout the Paleo community*, thanks to the nutrient-dense food advocacy of the Weston A. Price Foundation (WAPF).[9]

We understood the WAPF's message intellectually, but it took us awhile to get over our lifelong fear of fat and cholesterol, and to exchange our vegetable oils for lard and coconut oil. It took learning a little more about the science of why *saturated fats are so good for you.*

Humans need what are known as short- and medium-chain fatty acids, which are critical fuel for the brain, heart, and muscles. These are found in the fat of animals, not in processed vegetable oils. In addition, fats from pastured animals contain *Conjugated Linoleic Acid* (CLA) and high amounts of other *omega-3 fatty acids*—the very same ones doctors have been promoting for years via wild salmon and processed fish oil capsules.

> "The vital roles of these fat-soluble vitamins and the high levels found in the diets of healthy traditional peoples confirm the importance of pasture-feeding livestock. If domestic animals are not consuming green grass, vitamins A and K will be largely missing from their fat, organ meats, butterfat and egg yolks; if the animals are not raised in the sunlight, vitamin D will be largely missing from these foods."[8]
>
> **— Sally Fallon, co-author of *Nourishing Traditions* and President of WAPF**

33

Instead of taking daily omega-3 supplements, our family took a different approach. We looked into the ways in which we could easily and affordably add whole food sources into our diet. As a dairy-free family, we couldn't get it from butter. The logical progression became figuring out how to get healthful fat from our pastured hog, and that led us to lard. *The concept isn't a new one*; our grandmothers used lard long before manufacturers started pushing hydrogenated vegetable oils.

Crisco—Better than butter for cooking

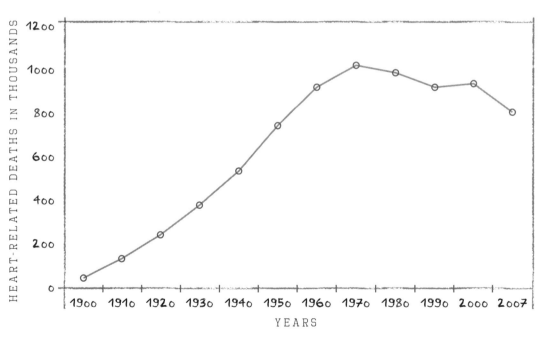

Right about now you're probably thinking: *Are these people trying to give me a heart attack?* Hardly. In fact, it was right around the time that all those hydrogenated vegetable oils began replacing lard that the incidence of heart disease in America shot up. **Think about that.**

Since we've been on the Paleo diet, our blood panels indicate that our family is in the best cardiovascular shape of our lives. Our serum cholesterol is down, our triglycerides are down, our HDL (good cholesterol) is up, and our blood pressure is down. All this in spite of greatly increasing our saturated fat and cholesterol intake! What happened to create this seeming paradox?

The link between ingesting cholesterol and saturated fat and heart disease is not as strong as you might think. We know, we know—it just seems so logical! If you put bacon grease down your drain, you clog your pipes. Shouldn't the same thing happen to your arteries? But studies don't back this up. Ancel Keys was behind the *Seven Countries Study*, the first and most famous study to find, among other things, an association between serum cholesterol and heart disease. The first results, published in the late fifties, highlighted the problem in the United States. What the study left out was the many other countries that didn't support their thesis. France, for example, has a high fat diet, but there is a low incidence of heart disease-related deaths; Finland has a relatively low fat intake, but a high incidence of heart-related deaths.

Yet despite this now disputed study, a high fat diet continues to be considered a cause of heart disease by a majority of Americans. *The assumption is that science still validates this correlation, but science has actually started leaning in the other direction.*

In the early 80s, another massive study scared people off fat and cholesterol. You may remember *Time* magazine's famous cover of a plate of eggs and bacon turned into a frowning face. The implication was that new research had proven that high cholesterol foods caused high cholesterol, which caused heart disease. What people failed to realize is that the study in question—*The Coronary Primary Prevention Trial*—was only attempting to correlate cholesterol in the blood with heart disease. In the study, they lowered blood cholesterol by administering a drug and were able to show that those that got the drug had a lower incidence of heart disease. The study makes no connection between dietary cholesterol and incidence of heart disease—or, for that matter, whether you should be worried about eating eggs and bacon.

> "Cholesterol level and saturated fat intake are not the major risk factors for heart disease."[11]
>
> – Mark Sisson, *The Primal Blueprint*

We can probably all agree that lowering serum cholesterol will lead to a decrease in heart disease risk. But does avoiding consumption of saturated fat lead to lower serum cholesterol or a lower risk of heart disease? Many studies have attempted to prove the link, but none have succeeded. A 2010 meta-analysis of all of the saturated fat studies showed that, overall, *there is no proven association between saturated fat intake and heart disease risk.*[10]

What can we conclude from all of this? That if there is a link between eating lard and bacon and fatty pork products and dying from a heart attack, it is not significant enough to be detected by medical science.

WHAT WE'RE LEFT WITH IS THE PREMISE OF THE PALEO DIET:

FOCUS ON EATING MEATS FROM HEALTHY ANIMALS AS WELL AS VEGETABLES, FRUITS, NUTS AND EGGS

THEN AVOID INFLAMMATION-CAUSING GRAINS, LEGUMES, PROCESSED DAIRY, AND REFINED SUGARS.

DOES PORK AFFECT YOUR BLOOD

When we decided to write a cookbook featuring only pork recipes, one of the most common responses we received was people mentioning that *they don't eat pork because of the recommendations of their favorite health guru.* The most common names that come up tend to be Paul Jaminet, author of *The Perfect Health Diet*, Joseph Mercola, and the Weston A. Price Foundation.

We read Jaminet's series,[12] the article on Mercola's site,[13] and the study published in the Weston A. Price Foundation journal *Wise Traditions*.[14] We did extensive research on the source material used for those recommendations, and consulted with a Ph.D. And guess what? We continue to feel that you have nothing to fear from eating pork, if you buy it wisely!

We recommend buying pork from reputable sources.

We actually met many of the pigs we consumed in the making of this book. They grew up in a clean environment, were handled in a humane way, and were slaughtered ethically. Ideally, you will be able to do the same. It's important to note that in the sources and studies used in any of the anti-pork crusades we read, the meat analyzed was from "immune-compromised" or CAFO pigs.

However, pigs are the animals that are least likely to get you sick. The impartial third party Centers for Science in Public Interest (CSPI) did a survey that looked at the relative incidence of sickness caused by various

food sources controlled for consumption and found that *pork was considerably safer than beef, poultry, or seafood.*[15]

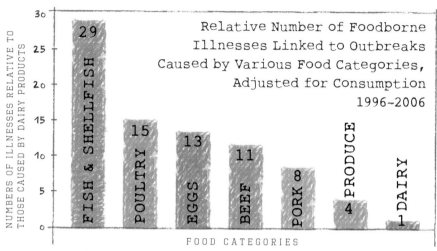

Using the yearly average illnesses linked to dairy outbreak as the baseline

Jaminet's argument[12] centers on zoonotic diseases, which are passed from animals to humans. Zoonotic diseases include mad cow disease and bird flu. In fact, almost all the animals that humans come in contact with (as pets or as livestock) are susceptible to these diseases. Jaminet was concerned with Hepatitis E (HEV). In particular, he references a study of CAFO pigs in China, which found that 4 percent of swine had HEV (not as high as we'd expect given the strong warnings). HEV has a *correlative* relationship with liver disease, hence the assumption of autoimmune disease and MS risk from pork consumption. Another study found that simply owning a pet, and not just consumption, increased that correlation. However, HEV is a 4-6 week self-limiting and self-resolving condition that only seriously threatens those already immune-compromised. Even if you are immune-compromised and get a rare case of HEV from pork, the resulting illness might be acute, but your body will quickly heal itself. All said, we agree with Jaminet's recommendation that people not eat raw liver or undercooked intestines of CAFO pigs.

The Mercola article[13] specifically addresses the commonality of pathogens discovered during a random survey among pork products. This, as clearly

indicated by the graph on the adjacent page, is not exclusive to pork—all CAFO-raised meats commonly carry pathogens. There is a very simple way to defeat these pathogens—cook your meat (see page 45 for information on proper pork cooking).

In 2011, the journal *Wise Traditions* published "How Does Pork Prepared in Various Ways Affect the Blood?"[14] The article was based on an experiment that attempted to prove unmarinated pork causes blood to congeal. Three participants were asked to consume marinated pork, cured pork, uncured bacon, and unmarinated pork; after five hours, blood was drawn from each and inspected under a microscope. The authors concluded that unmarinated and uncured pork caused blood cells to coagulate in potentially harmful ways.

The methods and analysis used in this study are too flawed to make sweeping conclusions about fresh pork. Science is a process, not a book of laws, and one study is never definitive. Furthermore, the trial was tiny—just three volunteers! They also used live blood analysis, a notoriously suspect technique. Here's what Dr. Sarah Ballantyne, biophysicist and author of *The Paleo Approach*, had to say about the study:

> There is a very good reason why live cell microscopy is not used by medical doctors (including those who specialize in blood disorders) nor by scientific researchers. Live blood analysis allows for subjectivity and is extremely sensitive to artefacts of blood collection and slide preparation. In the specific case of this study, the fibrin formation seen in the volunteer who ate fresh pork is a common artefact of blood on a glass slide (because glass is very good at causing fibrin to precipitate). Rouleaux and erythrocyte aggregation can simply be caused by allowing blood to sit a few extra seconds, especially if the sample is on the skimpy side, before covering the slide with a cover slip. There are too many variables to determine that the single volunteer's results reflect anything of a scientific nature in response to fresh pork consumption. This is the specific reason that published scientific studies only make any claims based on multiple measurement technique, multiple tests and multiple participants.

That said, if you still think marinated or cured meats are the only way to go, we have plenty of recipes for you. The majority of our dishes also incorporate lard, which is strongly encouraged by WAPF. For the rest of you, go ahead and eat your Perfect Pork Chops (page 170) pink and worry free.

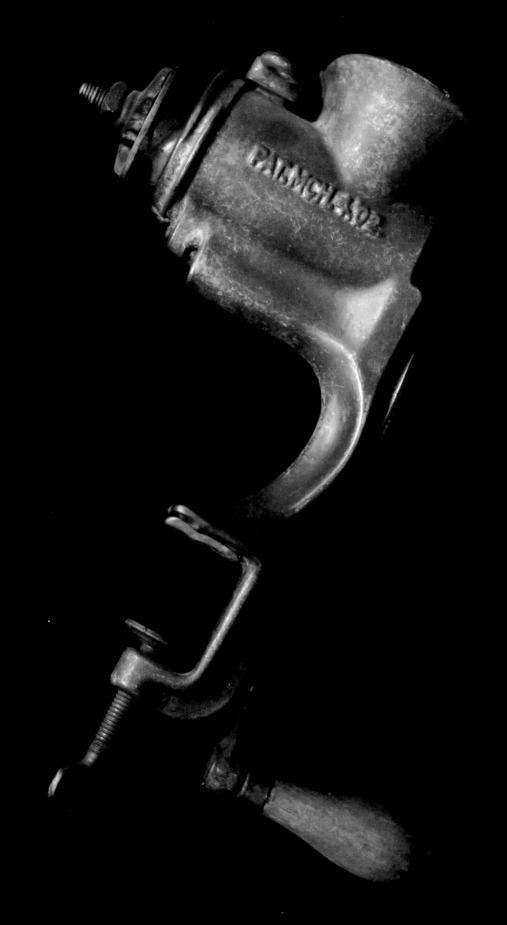

OUT WITH THE NEW AND IN WITH THE OLD

Just a few generations ago, the rates of heart disease, diabetes, and high cholesterol were much lower than they are today. Yet in most households, sausage and bacon were served every morning for breakfast, and lard was the first choice for pie crust. The decline in our health began with the introduction of transfatty acids (found in highly processed, oxidized, and bleached vegetable oils), as well as a new, genetically modified super-strain of wheat that enhanced the properties of gluten (the history of this is detailed very well in *Wheat Belly* by Dr. William Davis). This grain, although credited with saving entire countries from starvation and the scientist that developed it earned a Nobel Prize, has also correlated strongly with an increase in gluten intolerance and celiac disease. Add to that the increase in processed and refined foods—made more enticing with high-fructose corn syrup and phytoestrogenic soy—and you have our current health disaster. No one will argue that we have a crisis on our hands; the solution, we suggest, may be to get back to the food basics of previous generations.

"To me, life without veal stock, pork fat, sausage, organ meat, demi-glace, or even stinky cheese is a life not worth living."[16]

—Anthony Bourdain

Even with evidence to the contrary, plenty of people continue to believe that lard and fatty pork are part of the problem. Can they possibly be good for you to eat? Absolutely!

LOVE YOUR LARD, HUG YOUR HAM, and even LIKE YOUR LIVER!

The saturated and monounsaturated fats in animal fat are much more stable and less prone to oxidization than oil from corn, soybeans, grapeseed, or rapeseed (canola). Why is that good? Because less oxidation in oils means less oxidation in your blood stream, and that reduces the risk of inflammation and plaque in the arteries. The result of less inflammation is greater heart health and lower blood pressure.

It's worth repeating: Heart disease has risen steadily despite the popularization of low fat diets and vegetable, canola, and soybean oils.

Take a moment to think about how the majority of people in America eat. They grab a packaged frozen meal from the freezer and blast it in the microwave in plastic containers made with Bisephenol A (BPA), a compound so toxic it was finally banned from baby bottles here and in Canada. Do we really think that encourages health? Stacy's grandfather Art, who lived to be a feisty 95 years old, never ate any of that stuff (we can't bring ourselves to call it food). What was his secret?

For one thing, he, like our ancestors, ate those "awful" offal parts (heart, liver, tongue, etc.) that your grocery store doesn't even carry anymore. Most of us consider offal to be waste; we've never eaten those parts of the animals. But lately, trendy chefs at America's top restaurants have started featuring offal again; maybe they've realized something most of us have forgotten: An animal's internal organs have a lot of flavor. Better still, they are *powerful, nutrient-dense sources of vitamins and minerals we might not otherwise get.*

	Brain	Sweetbreads	Heart	Liver	Kidneys	Chitterlings	Bone Broth
Vitamin A				Excellent			
Vitamin C	Good			Great	Good		
Vitamin B12	Great	Excellent	Excellent	Excellent	Excellent	Good	
Riboflavin	Good	Good		Excellent	Excellent		
Niacin	Good		Great	Excellent	Great		
Thiamin	Good		Great	Good	Good		
Folate				Great			
Calcium							Great
Phosphorus	Great	Good	Good	Good	Good		Great
Selenium	Great	Excellent	Good	Excellent	Excellent	Good	
Iron		Good	Great	Excellent	Good		
Copper			Good	Great	Good		

Just look at how amazing liver is ... Truly the greatest superfood of all!

When it comes to nutrition, all organ meats beat muscle meat (that's the meat on the outside of the skeleton, like the ham or chop—in other words, what we most often consume). Generally, the organ you consume will help the part of your body you are trying to heal. For example, if you're looking for help with bone density, there's nothing better than marrow or a nutrient-packed bowl of bone broth.

How much organ meat should you consume? There's no one correct answer. If you enjoy it, eat as much as you want. We find we feel best when we're eating organ meats a few times a week and incorporate bone broth several times a week. In other words, you don't need to serve liver daily to reap the benefits!

"It's only polite really if you knock an animal on the head to eat it all: tripe, heart, feet, ears, head, tail. It's all good stuff."[17]

—Fergus Henderson, author of *The Whole Beast: Nose to Tail Eating*

WILL PINK PORK KILL ME?

When we were growing up, our mothers cooked pork like it was chicken: *well done*. That's because the USDA decided pink pork was the cause of potential pathogens, particularly the trichina worm. They recommended cooking pork all the way through, to an internal temperature of 160°F. The result—Dry pork chops for everyone!

But when the USDA later traced the source of the contamination,[6] they discovered it primarily had to do with the way the pigs were cooked after they died. It had to do with the raw meat scraps pigs ate when they were alive. That is now illegal. As a result, the incidence of trichinosis infection has dropped to near zero in the U.S.; the few cases left are mostly caused by the consumption of undercooked game, not pork.[6]

The USDA now recommends only a minimum internal temperature of 145°F for all pork muscle meats, including roasts, tenderloins, and chops. This is the equivalent of *medium rare* for a steak. Offal meats and ground pork should still be cooked through to 160°F.

	TEMPERATURE TO REACH	COULD IT BE PINK?
GROUND MEAT	160 degrees	No
ORGAN MEATS	160 degrees	No
SMOKED PORK	185 degrees	No
PORK CHOPS AND ROASTS	145 degrees	Yes

The above chart will help you keep track of ideal cooking temperatures for various cuts of pork, but we also specify temperatures in each recipe, unless the meat is slow-roasted or braised. The fat and connective tissue-rich cuts found in barbecue, for example, should be cooked beyond 160°F.

If you still prefer to cook all of your pork to 160°F, take care not to overcook it! In particular, roasts and chops dry out at higher temperatures.

Also keep in mind that pastured meats are more fragile than conventional pork and can be ruined much faster.

If nothing else, let's keep dry pork chops where they belong— back in the '80s.

WHAT WE MEAN BY "QUALITY" INGREDIENTS

While you can *make your own bacon* (see page 68), most of you will not. So here's how to navigate the confusing world of buying bacon.

First and foremost, always choose thick cut if it's available. All of the recipes in *Beyond Bacon* were created with thick cut bacon—to us, it's just more meaty and delicious.

Bacon comes in two varieties: cured and uncured. Bacon (and pancetta and prosciutto and ham) must be cured with sodium nitrate or sodium nitrite, which is naturally pink and therefore called pink salt. If your bacon says uncured, it simply means that the nitrate content is coming from something other than salt crystals, usually beet powder or celery juice. Sodium nitrate is the most effective and tastiest way to eliminate bacteria, especially the super-toxic botulinum.

Your ingredients list should be limited to pork, salt, sugar (or brown sugar or maple sugar), and spices. Any additional ingredients are bad news. In our recipes, we use sea salt with naturally-occurring nitrates, but you can choose to substitute beet extract or even Instacure #2. If you're concerned about sodium, we find that quality pork products with naturally occurring ingredients (sodium nitrate being one) have no ill effect on our bodies. But you need to decide what works best for you. The same goes for sugar, which gets a lot of people nervous. Bacon only ends up with 1-2 grams of sugar per serving, and that's not much at all (an apple has over 20 grams of sugar). Besides, bacon just doesn't taste like bacon without a sweetener.

You should also make sure that your bacon is gluten free. Bacon and wheat do not belong together, which hasn't stopped larger brands from adding it! So read the ingredients carefully.

Finally, we recommend that your bacon be smoked. See what wood is referenced on the packaging. Hickory? Apple wood? Mesquite? These are all terrific flavors.

BACON AND NITRATES

"I had rather be shut up in a very modest cottage with my books, my family and a few old friends, dining on simple bacon, and letting the world roll on as it liked, than to occupy the most splendid post, which any human power can give."[18]

—Thomas Jefferson

SAUSAGE

Once again, look for a clean ingredients list: *just pork, salt, and spices.*

Preservatives are not necessary because the salt content in sausage is so high. But, companies love to add chemicals. To be on the safe side, why not stuff your own? Sausages are a lot easier to make than bacon, and ground pork is very affordable. Not to mention, then you can avoid the sweeteners that are in almost all pre-prepared sausages.

FLOURS

When we gave up wheat, we also gave up the convenience of wheat flour. Stacy suffers from celiac disease, which means that wheat poisons her system. Wheat flour baking is difficult to mimic since gluten itself is a protein binder like no other. To replace it, we often *combine four different kinds of flour.*

Our first love is *almond flour,* made from pulverized blanched almond nuts. It's very flavorful, high in protein and fat but not starch, and lends a rich taste to food. For delicate baked goods, try Honeyville Blanched Almond Flour.

We also use *coconut flour,* which is dried coconut flesh pulverized into a powder. This flour has fat and protein, but also a large amount of dietary fiber. It is important to use a fine grain coconut flour (available in specialty grocery and health foods stores), not shredded coconut, which is much coarser and unsuitable for the recipes in this book.

For recipes that require starch, we use *tapioca flour* (sometimes called tapioca starch) and *arrowroot powder* (sometimes called arrowroot starch). Both are dried and powdered tubers, which means that they are high in complex carbohydrates. These are much lighter in weight than almond or coconut flours. Arrowroot powder, in particular, is excellent for thickening sauces in place of wheat flour or cornstarch. You can find both of these in the health section of supermarkets, in your local co-op, as well as online and in Asian markets.

We know we'll get some flack for including granulated sugar in some of our recipes. We understand the misgivings. To be clear, we only use *unrefined sugars, which have naturally occurring nutrients and are lower on the glycemic index than refined sugar.*

When a recipe does call for granulated sugar, it's because liquid won't work. We prefer palm, date, and maple granulated sugar. Date sugar is made from dried dates and is ground super fine. Palm sugar comes from sugar palm or coconut sap and maple sugar is from the sap of the sugar maple tree; in both cases, the sap is boiled until it is very thick and then cooled. All of these are naturally occurring and minimally processed.

SUGAR

Flipping through this book, you'll find *plenty of interesting spices* —from the mundane (cinnamon and paprika) to the more exotic (mace and cardamom).

All of the ground spices are available at your local grocery store or co-op right next to the salt and pepper. A few recipes include whole spices, like allspice berries and star anise pods. These may be harder to find, but they are certainly available online, and in Asian markets and spice stores.

We recognize that good quality spices can be expensive, especially organic ones. Spices enhance flavor, but none of them are integral to the integrity of the dish. So if you can't afford or find fennel seeds, leave them out!

SPICES

We cook with a *variety of salts from around the world* (Himalayan Pink and Hawaiian Red Salt are our favorites) and keep a finishing sea salt on the table.

We also enjoy sea salt mixed with powdered kelp (sea vegetable salt), which adds iodine and a slight flavor of the sea. Experiment and find what works best for you.

SALT

What
Tools Do
I Use?

FRYER

We use a small electric fryer for deep-frying. While it is possible to use a heavy-bottomed pot instead, this smaller appliance offers a lot of advantages. First, once you set your temperature, you can rely on the automatic cycling of the fryer to keep it steady. A pot of oil requires constant attention to prevent burning. Second, it's probably safer. Electric fryers have breakaway cords and lids that help to prevent grease fires and serious burns. Hot oil is dangerous!

ICE CREAM MAKER

The way to make ice cream has been unchanged for hundreds of years: continually stir a sweetened milk/cream mixture in a below freezing carafe so that tiny, melt-on-your-tongue ice crystals form. Without a way to continually churn or a way to drop your temperature below freezing, you can't make ice cream! Luckily modern ice cream makers make it easy with an electric motor and freezable carafe.

ELECTRIC MIXER

For baking we swear by our stand mixer. It not only makes beating eggs and blending flours a cinch, the attachments—like the meat grinder and sausage stuffer—make lots of other things quick and easy, too. Do you really want to spend 15 minutes hand-whipping egg whites for our Spinach & Bacon Soufflé (page 232) or Baconnaise (page 256)? Or do you want to do it in three minutes easily?

MEAT GRINDER/ SAUSAGE STUFFER

We've started to think of our meat grinder—an attachment for our stand mixer—as a kitchen essential. The quality of our lard would diminish dramatically without the grinder, which can mince the fat into the tiniest of pieces. We also use it to incorporate liver and kidneys into our ground meat dishes. Once we added a stuffing funnel to the end of the grinder, we were amazed at how easy it was to stuff sausages into casings. A meat grinder isn't absolutely necessary—a good food processor will get your meat tiny enough and a piping bag will certainly stuff a sausage—but it has certainly improved the efficiency of our kitchen!

FOOD PROCESSOR

Of all the tools in our kitchen, this one has saved us the most time. Whether the food processor is grating carrots and papaya for our Green Papaya Salad with Poached Jowl (page 204), or puréeing the ingredients for our Rosemary Carrot Mash (page 220), it will save you from the most torturously time-consuming tasks. Yes, you could use a box grater, a knife, or a potato masher, but surely you have better things to do with your time!

BLENDER/ IMMERSION BLENDER

There are some who swear by their blenders, using it for every task in food prep. We were given a super high-speed blender, but we don't use it much. The best task for a blender is puréeing soups, like our Acorn Squash Soup with Crispy Lardons (page 118), or sauces, like our Liver Gravy (page 252). If you want one, there's no need to spend hundreds of dollars on a fancy model; any cheap blender, or even an immersion blender (the kind you submerge into the soup or sauce), will do.

DEHYDRATOR

When we first started eating grass-fed meat, we got a dehydrator to make jerky. Little did we know how many different uses we'd get out of it! You can make fruit leather, bake cookies, and preserve vegetables, among many other things. In this book, we use it to make Curried Cracklin's (page 192); turns out it's the perfect tool for eliminating all the moisture from pork skin, which is what makes it puff up when you fry it. If you don't have a dehydrator, an oven at its lowest setting will work, though with no fan to circulate the air the process will take much, much longer.

How Do I Get STARTED?

Some of the things we'll talk about in the book require unique cooking techniques—as in stuff you wouldn't normally try at home. Special tools will be involved, but, rest assured, you can accomplish all of them. At the very least, we will make it easy enough that you can *have fun trying something new,* whether it's smoking pork or stuffing your own sausages!

"Everything in food is science. The only subjective part is when you eat it."[19]

—Alton Brown

SMOKING

Real barbecues are gigantic pits of smoke, fire, and coals. They look intimidating—not like something you could just up and create yourself. And while it's true that using hard wood in a real pit is probably the best way to experience barbecue, it is by no means the only way. You can do it at home. You don't need much beyond a kettle charcoal smoker, which, when compared to the price of your gas grill, is cheap.

Smoking meat is simple once you get the hang of it. The first step is to buy smoking chips. We've found apple wood chips in regular grocery stores and more exotic woods in barbecue stores or online. Different wood chips impart a different flavor, so you should experiment to see what you like best. You'll want to first soak the chips in water for at least thirty minutes; this is so they will smolder rather than catch fire. Light your charcoal in the bottom of your smoker and wait until they become hot coals; this takes between 15 and 30 minutes. The top of your grill should be at between 250-275°F when closed.

Put your soaked chips in the smoking basket and your meat on the top racks. (For a colder smoke for bacon and other cured meats, put the chips directly on top of the coals.) We like to season our meat with dry rubs and have included several recipes, but you might prefer wet sauces. The choice is yours.

If buying a new piece of equipment is too expensive for you, *you can build one for yourself with* just a large terracotta pot, a large terracotta bowl, a hot plate, and a round grill rack. Here's how to construct it:

1. Raise the pot off the ground with some bricks but leave the hole at the bottom of the pot uncovered for the hot plate cord.

2. Place the hot plate in the bottom of the pot, and pull the hot plate cord through the hole so you can plug it into an outlet or extension cord. Put your soaked wood chips into an aluminum pie plate and put that on top of the hot plate.

3. Place the grill rack on top of the pot so that it sits inside the pot, but well above the hot plate.

4. Cover with the bowl, which is your lid.

5. Turn on the hot plate and you're smoking!

Can you smoke meat with a regular gas grill?
We've done it, and it's effective if not perfect. If you want to try it, here's how:

1. Put your soaked wood chips in a pie plate and cover the top tightly with aluminum foil. With a butter knife, poke about ten holes in the foil.

2. Remove the grates from one side of your grill and place the pie plate directly on those burners.

3. Light your grill and set only the burners underneath the wood chips on their lowest setting.

4. If there is a large vent on the side of the grill with the wood chips, plug it with an old rag to prevent the smoke from escaping.

5. Keep your meat on the opposite side of the grill, where the grates are still in place. Wait for the wood to start smoking—at least 15 minutes—before you place your meat on the grill.

This is an unsophisticated version of smoking, and real pit masters frown on it, but we've done it many times. The taste is not as intense as what you'll get from the first two methods, but the meat is still tender and delicious.

Smoking is very rewarding. It just takes a little patience, some know-how, and top-quality meat. Good luck!

DEEP FRYING

The idea of eating fried foods might give your doctor a heart attack, so maybe keep this section between us. Just know that our family is in great health after eating fried foods regularly. And besides, didn't we already tell you that *everything you were taught about saturated fat was wrong?*

Despite what you may think, frying food is not about adding fat to it. The intention is to keep the meat as moist as possible while turning the outside crisp. That means cooking as quickly as possible using liquid that can heat to super high temperatures before evaporating or burning. We use lard because it won't smoke or burn at 350 and 375°F temperatures, and because it provides a neutral, yet rich flavor that compliments some of our favorite recipes. If you do not have large quantities of lard on hand, coconut oil works, too.

What's the best way to fry? Electric fryers are the smartest option because they maintain the correct temperature and have safety features that minimize accidents. You can find them online at most places where small appliances are sold.

Frying in a heavy-bottomed or cast-iron pot can also work, but it takes more effort and concentration. You'll definitely need a thermometer to monitor the temperature of the oil. If your lard gets hotter than 375°F, it may start to smoke and burn and ruin the food.

You need just enough lard or coconut oil to submerge your meat. This usually works out to a few inches up the side of the pot. Do not use more than that. You'll want to heat your oil slowly. We recommend setting your burner to medium-low, only raising the heat if the temperature plateaus before you reach 350-375°F. Once it reaches frying temperature, watch the thermometer and reduce the heat if it gets too hot.

Whatever method you use, put your food in the hot oil carefully! We use a Chinese spider or tongs to place each piece of meat in the fryer. You do not want to splash yourself; the oil will be incredibly hot—much worse than hot coffee. For this reason, never, ever let young children help you with frying.

Once the meat is done frying, the pieces need to be drained. Remember, you're going for crispy, not greasy! Remove the food from the oil and place it on a couple of towels spread on a plate (you've probably done this for bacon); you can also lay a clean dishtowel or clean rag on a drying rack.

Don't throw out the remaining oil! You can use it to fry again. Take a fine mesh strainer or several layers of cheesecloth, filter the oil into an airtight storage container, and stick it in the fridge or freezer. The oil can be reused a half dozen times; just add a bit of fresh oil each time and strain well once finished. Discard the entire batch if it becomes discolored or smokes during heating.

Happy frying! I hope that when using these recipes, you too will learn the joys of frying!

SAUSAGE STUFFING

Before we started researching this book, we honestly thought that stuffing sausages at home was impossible. We made our own sausage patties, but had never attempted links. Surprisingly, we found *it couldn't be simpler if you have the right tools and ingredients.*

The casing we recommend you stuff your meat into is made from the intestine of the pig. That makes a lot of people squeamish, but think about it—if you've been eating store-bought sausages for years, you've been eating hog intestines. Don't worry, the casings you will be purchasing will be thoroughly cleaned and odor free. They are packed in salt (as a preservative), which means they will last far longer than any meat product. And since few people make sausages these days, they are also cheap!

The first step is to cut off a length of hog casing for each sausage, or one very long casing if you are making links; you will need about twice the length of the sausage you intend to make since the casings shrink as they are stuffed. Brush off as much salt as you can, and soak the casings in cold water.

After you prepare the sausage meat in our recipes, you'll need to set up a stuffing funnel. The easiest way to stuff sausages is to use an attachment for a meat grinder; this will push the meat through evenly. We use the sausage attachment that came with our KitchenAid stand mixer.

Find the end of your hog casing and place the opening over the end of the funnel. Push the length of the casing up on to the funnel, wriggling it evenly so that the entire length is gathered on the funnel except for the very end.

Push the meat through to the tip of the funnel tube before closing the casing's end with a knot. If you tie the casing before the meat is at the tip of the funnel, you will have yourself a sausage link of air instead of meat. When ready, slowly push the meat into the casing, being sure to fill the casing completely before dispensing more casing from the funnel. Fill the casing, but not so tight that the sausage is strained or bursting. If the casing is too full, you're guaranteed a broken sausage when it cooks.

To create a link, pause in pushing the sausage meat and twist the casing several times where you want a new link to begin. When your meat has been stuffed, tie a knot at the end of the last link and cut off the excess.

Can you still do this if you don't have a meat grinder or sausage stuffer? Absolutely! The most effective and brilliant technique is using a pastry bag with the inner ring inserted, but without a tip. With this set up, the casing is bunched up around the plastic end of the bag and the sausage is slowly extruded into the casing by squeezing the bag.

Sausage stuffing is a great adventure. Give it a try!

In this section, you'll find the basic techniques for most of our recipes. The principles behind the way we cook and eat extend back to ancient times, when humans needed to extract as much nutrition as possible from a single animal, then preserve the meat for extended periods of time. There's a functional reason for many of the tastiest things people eat. You like bacon because it's delicious, but our ancestors cured pig belly so the meat would last for weeks instead of days. Meat stock was simply a way to suck every last bit of nourishment from bones. Lard is the conversion of fat into something stable that could sit on a shelf. And salty sausages were a good way of making preserved meat portable.

Curing our own bacon and pancetta with minimal nitrate content, rendering pork fat into lard, and stuffing our own sausage casings has allowed us to move away from buying pork in stores. But if this doesn't work for you, don't worry. You can substitute store-bought chicken or beef stock in a carton for the homemade pork stock in our recipes; just be sure to buy brands free of monosodium glutamate and gluten! It's always best to procure bacon from a local pig farmer or butcher, but if you can only buy bacon in a grocery store, opt for uncured. Sausages are usually a staple of any farmers' market, butcher, or farmer who sells directly to consumers.

Lard, however, is different. If you buy it in a store, it will be full of preservatives and, likely, a hydrogenated monstrosity. So try your local butcher or pork farmer; they can probably sell you rendered lard. If you are unable to get clean lard, use pastured butter or palm shortening (not coconut oil) for baking and coconut oil for frying.

The BASICS: Lard, Stock, Sausages & Cured Meats

Our very favorite cooking oil isn't oil at all: *it's fat.* Pork fat has amazing flavor and we use it for almost everything. Best of all? Unlike canola oil or vegetable oil, you can make it at home! All it takes is some solid pork fat and a little time.

There are two types of fat you can purchase: leaf fat or back fat. *Leaf fat* is from the area surrounding the pig's kidneys, inside the abdomen. *Back fat* is just under the skin. If you are unsure of what you have, leaf fat is more crumbly and generally doesn't come in wide sheets like back fat. Leaf lard doesn't have the slightly porky taste of lard made from back fat, so it is best for baking. Back fat lard is perfect for cooking.

> "Rich in Vitamin D and heat-stable, this traditional fat is a top-pick of mine for cooking and nutrients... Lard is also one of our richest dietary sources of Vitamin D, a nutrient that's so tough to get from food—and from climates that lack sunshine year-round—that many doctors and nutritionists today now recommend that people take it as a supplement."[20]
>
> **-Diane Sanfilippo, author of *Practical Paleo***

RENDERING YOUR OWN LARD

While the process of making lard is simple, it is also easy to ruin. Often, people render lard in crockpots, which we don't recommend. Crockpots make it easy to forget about your fat, and you need to watch it closely as it renders. You definitely can't leave it overnight; before we knew better, we burned large batches of lard from the carryover heat of an unplugged crockpot.

How do you know if your lard is burned and ruined? Well, look at the picture of the two lards. *Pure and clean lard will solidify snow white.* Burned lard is a brownish-yellow color; it will taste bitter and ruin your food. Don't use it!

Rendering lard does smell a bit. It's not as unpleasant as chitterlings or even beef tallow, but it is permeating and strong. If you have an electric burner attached to your grill outside, you could render your lard there, but promise us you'll keep an eye on it!

RENDERING YOUR OWN LARD

DIFFICULTY
Basic

TIME to TABLE
2 hours

YIELD
Makes about 2½ pints

EQUIPMENT
Large pot with lid

INGREDIENTS
4 pounds pork fat (either back fat or leaf fat)

1. Grind, slice, or process fat into the smallest pieces you can achieve. Grinding is best, as the smaller the pieces, the more lard you will render.

2. Transfer the fat to the pot, and cook on low, stirring occasionally. You will notice that the lard begins to emerge as a liquid. Every 30 minutes, pour and strain the lard out with a fine mesh strainer. It is preferred that you do this frequently so that the rendered lard is retained in case the remaining fat accidentally burns and ruins any lard still in the pot.

3. When the fat begins to turn golden brown, you are approaching the end of the rendering. Pour out and strain the lard. Bottle the strained lard in sealable mason jars.

4. If the fat turns dark brown, it is burned. Any lard in the pot will be burned and will taste bitter. Discard this fat and lard; unfortunately it cannot be salvaged.

5. Save the remaining meaty pieces to make Crispy Lardons (page 190), which taste like bacon!

> "No self-respecting French chef would ever be without lard. Leaf lard is obtained from the visceral fat deposit surrounding the kidney and loin, and is considered the highest grade of lard because it has little pork flavor. This is why it's prized in baking, where it's used to make flaky, moist pie crusts, croissants, and other non-Paleo delights. Lard is an incredibly versatile fat. I use it mostly to roast vegetables. Unlike olive oil, vegetables roasted in lard do not get soggy or greasy. They stay crisp and almost dry, with a wonderful flavor. This surprises people because they think of lard as 'greasy.' Not so. A tablespoon of lard has about 6g MFA, 5g SFA and 1.6g PUFA."[21]
>
> **—Chris Kresser, L.Ac**

DIFFICULTY
Basic

TIME TO TABLE
Less than 24 hours

YIELD
Makes up to 64 ounces

EQUIPMENT
Large stockpot

INGREDIENTS

3 pounds pork bones

1 tablespoon salt

1 tablespoon peppercorns

1 tablespoon apple cider
vinegar

Note: You will find that a lot of scum rises to the top of pork stock. It tastes bitter and is unpalatable, so just skim it off. Our alternative technique is to start off with just the bones in water, bring the water to a boil and let them cook for five minutes, then dump out the water. Put the bones back in fresh water, add the other ingredients, and proceed with cooking. Your final stock will be less scummy.

You've probably seen and used cartons of beef and chicken stock. You may have used fish stock as well. Pork stock, however, is pretty rare, and that's a shame! It's an excellent base for soups and tastes great on its own. As one of our friends said, *"Pork stock, where have you been all my life?"*

People tend to opt for beef or chicken stock because of pork's higher fat content; *fatty stocks do not make great soups.* But this is easily solved by refrigerating your pork stock and skimming the fat off the top.

You can make pork stock in a big pot or in a *crockpot or a pressure cooker.* If using a crockpot, double the time indicated in the recipe; if using a pressure cooker, halve the time. And don't toss the bones when you're done; you can boil them again. You'll get diminishing returns in terms of nutritional content and flavor each time you reuse the bones, but they will still make a delicious stock.

PORK STOCK

1. Put all of the bones in the pot, and cover them completely with water.

2. Cook on high until the water comes to a boil and scum rises to the top, about 5 minutes.

3. Dump the entire pot of scummy water, and begin again, this time adding the salt, peppercorns, and vinegar to the water. Once it comes to a boil, reduce the heat to low and cover.

4. Simmer for at least 9 hours, or up to 24 hours. The longer you cook it, the more nutrient value you will extract from the bones.

5. Remove the pot from the heat, and strain the stock. Place the stock in a large airtight container and refrigerate to chill overnight.

6. Skim the fat off the top of the stock, and transfer the rest to storage containers. Mason jars are an excellent way to save the stock; they are airtight and can be used for freezing. Just make sure there is a small amount of room is left in the jar to allow for the expansion of the liquid as it freezes.

DIFFICULTY
Advanced

TIME to TABLE
More than a day

SERVES
1-10, depending on your love of bacon

EQUIPMENT
Smoker or grill

INGREDIENTS

2½ pounds pork belly, skin removed (save it for Curried Cracklin's, page 192)

2 cups pink sea salt (or 1⅞ cup salt and 2 tablespoons curing salt)

1 cup granulated maple, date, or palm sugar

6 cups water

1 tablespoon crushed black peppercorns

If you're Paleo, you've read a lot about the amazing flavors of bacon, also known as "*meat candy.*" At anywhere from 6 to 15 dollars a pound for the good stuff, it can be a very expensive habit. So why not cure and smoke your own? Granted, it's a long and complicated process, thanks to the smoking involved, but the results are worth it. Also worth it: making a lot at once so you'll be set for a *while.* Imagine the pride you'll feel munching on your very own slice of *salty-smoky heaven!* There's no contest between the taste of homemade and store bought brands.

MAKE YOUR OWN BACON

1. In a bowl or dish large enough to hold the pork, whisk together the water, salt, sugar, and pepper until the salt and sugar are fully dissolved. This will be your brine.

2. Fully submerge the pork belly in the brine, using smaller bowls with canned goods on top to weigh them down, if necessary. It is important that no part of the pork belly is out of the brining mixture.

3. Cover the dish, and transfer it to the refrigerator. Allow the brining bowl with pork belly to chill and cure for five days. You don't need an airtight seal since the meat is fully submerged. Check on the pork each subsequent day until the belly feels as though you are pushing on a well-inflated basketball. This process could take up to a week.

4. Once ready, rinse the bacon and prepare a colder smoke at a temperature of 200°F. Follow the instructions on page 54, but this time, place your wood chips (hickory, apple wood, and even mesquite are all used to impart that smoky flavor) directly on the coals. If using an alternative method, follow the procedure as described.

5. Smoke for about 3 hours or until the bacon reaches an internal temperature of 150°F. (This temperature will impart all the smoky flavor and kill any remaining bacteria, but will allow for further frying or cooking in dishes.)

6. Depending on your taste preferences, you may find the bacon to be too salty. If that is the case, simmer slices you wish to use in a pot of boiling water for 1 minute just before using. Then, dry the bacon, and fry it as you normally would.

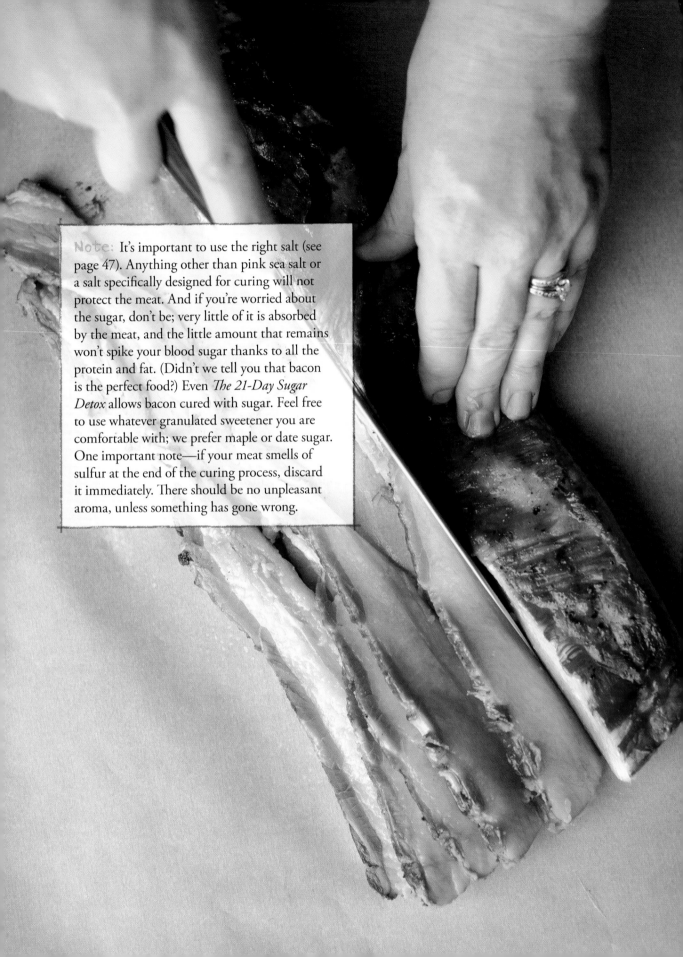

Note: It's important to use the right salt (see page 47). Anything other than pink sea salt or a salt specifically designed for curing will not protect the meat. And if you're worried about the sugar, don't be; very little of it is absorbed by the meat, and the little amount that remains won't spike your blood sugar thanks to all the protein and fat. (Didn't we tell you that bacon is the perfect food?) Even *The 21-Day Sugar Detox* allows bacon cured with sugar. Feel free to use whatever granulated sweetener you are comfortable with; we prefer maple or date sugar. One important note—if your meat smells of sulfur at the end of the curing process, discard it immediately. There should be no unpleasant aroma, unless something has gone wrong.

DIFFICULTY
Advanced

TIME TO TABLE
More than a day

YIELD
Several meals

EQUIPMENT
Kitchen twine,
a dark, cool room

INGREDIENTS

1 teaspoon dried thyme

1 teaspoon dried rosemary

1 teaspoon dried marjoram

½ teaspoon paprika

2 dried bay leaves, minced

2 teaspoons black peppercorns, crushed

2½ pounds pork belly, skin removed (save it for Curried Cracklin's, page 192)

¼ cup pink sea salt (or 3 tablespoons salt and 1 tablespoon curing salt)

Note: When you refrigerate your cured Pancetta, it can last up to several weeks.

Pancetta, also known as *"Italian bacon,"* is pork belly cured like bacon, but not smoked. It is also savory—flavored with *herbs and spices* rather than sweetened. We really enjoy the flavor differences between pancetta and bacon and alternate between the two in our recipes. In fact, you can always substitute pancetta for any recipe with chopped bacon—it's great in *Apple & Bacon Stuffed Pork Chops* (page 168) and *Zucchini Pasta with Avocado, Roasted Tomato & Bacon* (page 234).

MAKE YOUR OWN PANCETTA

1. In a small bowl, create a rub by mixing the thyme, rosemary, marjoram, paprika, bay leaves, and crushed peppercorns until evenly distributed. Coat the pork belly with this mixture.

2. Coat the pork belly on all sides with the salt, and then layer on more of the herb mixture.

3. Place the pork in a plastic ziplock bag, and remove as much of the air as possible. If you do not have a vacuum sealer, place a straw in the bag, zip it closed except for where the straw emerges, and suck out all of the air with the straw before removing the straw and sealing the bag. Place this bag in the refrigerator.

4. Wait several days for the belly to lose moisture. Check on it each day until the belly can no longer be squeezed from the outside of the bag (do not open it). As you push on it, it should feel firm, as though you are touching a flexed muscle. This process could take up to a week.

5. Brush or wipe off the excess salt and herbs from the pork. Fresh herbs left on the pork may cause mold, so make sure they are all removed.

6. Once the pork is dried and clean, lay it fat side down, and roll it into a cylindrical shape by rolling it inward as tightly as you can. The more airtight the roll, the better it will hold its shape once completed. Tie it tightly with several strands of kitchen twine, leaving enough twine on one end to hang the meat so that it is not touching anything.

7. Place your meat in a cool, dry, and dark place like a basement closet. Leave it there for a week. Don't forget about it; set a calendar reminder if need be!

8. At the end of the week, your pancetta may have browned slightly on the outside, but that is normal. It should be very firm to the touch and will not unroll when the strings are removed.

9. Depending on taste preferences, you may find it to be too salty. If that is the case, simply simmer slices or cubes you wish to use in a pot of boiling water for 1 minute. Then, dry it and fry it as you normally would.

Note: As with bacon, it's important to use the right salt. Anything other than pink sea salt or a salt specifically designed for curing will not protect the meat. Those with concerns about sodium nitrate should refer to our bacon section, on page 47. Since light and warmth will lead to spoilage, make sure you have a dark, cool place to store the meat for a week. If at the end of the curing period your meat has an aroma of any kind, especially sulfur, discard immediately.

DIFFICULTY
Intermediate

TIME to TABLE
6-12 hours

SERVES
10-12

EQUIPMENT
Meat grinder or food processor

INGREDIENTS

1 meaty pork skull, cheeks, tongue, and jowls removed

2 bay leaves

1 tablespoon peppercorns

1 tablespoon salt

2 tablespoon gelatin powder

1 teaspoon ground nutmeg

1 teaspoon ground dry mustard

1 teaspoon dried parsley

½ teaspoon ground allspice

½ teaspoon cayenne pepper

½ teaspoon white pepper

Note: For the squeamish, creating this was not as hard as you might think. After adding the water and putting it on the heat, we hardly had to look at it until it couldn't look back at us!

Stacy's grandfather used to go on long rants about the head cheese of his youth and how he hadn't had any good head cheese in so very long. The entire family (including us) was grossed out at the idea and always gave him a hard time about it. At one point, we found it online for him and watched the man devour plain cold slices, a whole pound's worth. It was then we set out on *a mission to perfect this dish* for him, despite an honest hesitation on our part to even try. After all, we hadn't been brave enough to taste the one we'd purchased.

HEAD CHEESE

1. Place the butchered pork skull (not including removed parts) in a very large stockpot. If your stockpot is not large enough to fit the skull, you may need to have your butcher quarter it. To be clear, the brain can and should be included with the skull. I know it may be creepy, but brain is an incredibly high source of DHA, as well as selenium. Most people have a selenium deficiency because it's hard to find. Since it melts into the pot of water, you will never know it was there!

2. Add enough water to fill the pot, saving a few inches at the top so that it doesn't boil over. Add the bay leaves, peppercorns, and salt. Then, cover the pot, if you can, and bring the water to a boil on high heat.

3. Allow the water to boil for several hours until the remaining meat comes loose from the bones, and the skull is clean. This may take 4-5 hours.

4. Remove and discard the skull and mandible (which should have disconnected from the softening of the bones) and any remaining bones (or reserve all bones to make Pork Stock, page 66). Strain, and reserve the cooking liquid. Remove the bay leaves.

5. Grind or chop the strained meat in a food processor or meat grinder to a large ground meat consistency, and place it in a large mixing bowl. This is optional, as traditional head cheese uses larger chunks of meat. But our personal preference is a more meatloaf-like texture to please the palate.

6. In a large bowl, mix 2 cups of the cooking liquid with the ground meat and gelatin. When thoroughly combined, add the nutmeg, mustard, parsley, allspice, cayenne pepper, and white pepper, and mix again.

7. Line a loaf pan with parchment or wax paper, and transfer the head cheese to the loaf pan. Refrigerate for 4 hours, or until firm.

8. To serve, remove the head cheese from the loaf pan, and slice it. You can serve it on slices of cucumber or tomato, fresh herbs, or alongside morning eggs. It's a wonderful conversation piece at parties, and most people will give anything a try at least once!

HEAD CHEESE

What we found as the dreaded recipe testing for this eventually *awesome and nutrient-dense dish* approached, was a friend in the local butcher. Don from The Organic Butcher of McLean graciously butchered the head for us at no additional cost to the least expensive cut of meat we had ever purchased. From it we saved the tongue (for *Lengua Carnitas*, page 144), Jowl (for *Green Papaya Salad*, page 204), Neck (*Braised Neck Roast*, page 130), glands (*Sweetbreads*, page 194), snout (*Acorn Squash Soup with Crispy Lardons*, page 118), ears and skin (*Cracklin's*, page 192) and a bunch of ground meat! If you're looking for affordable cuts of meat, this by far and away cannot be beat. And since the butcher took care of the hard work, all we had to do was put some bones in a pot to boil—which we do all the time for *Pork Stock* (page 66) anyway!

When Stacy shared this recipe with her grandfather, before he passed, we were thrilled to hear him say, *"It's very good, and you should definitely put it in your book and be proud."*

DIFFICULTY
Advanced

TIME TO TABLE
6-12 hours

YIELD
More than 2 dozen

EQUIPMENT
Meat grinder or food processor

INGREDIENTS

4 trotters

1 pork liver (about ½ pound)

1 pork heart (about ½ pound)

1½ cup tapioca flour

1½ cup arrowroot powder

2½ cups blanched almond flour

3 tablespoons salt

1 teaspoon pepper

2 teaspoons marjoram

1 teaspoon mace

1 teaspoon onion powder

1 tablespoon gelatin powder

Almond flour for dusting

2 tablespoons Lard (page 62)

Many years ago, when Stacy was a vegetarian, her father bet her 50 dollars that she wouldn't eat scrapple, a dish he loved. Her dad wouldn't touch *head cheese*, but he *loved scrapple*—go figure! Stacy held her nose, swallowed the scrapple, and got the 50 bucks. Never did she think she would be making a recipe for it some day! We have since made it our mission to do our own take on this food her father loves. Now Stacy eats it without holding her nose. In fact, we regularly devour a big batch for breakfast! It's a *super tasty way* to get your recommended organ meats.

The loaves in this recipe freeze well; just thaw them in the fridge before you plan to cook them. We like to dust the slices with almond flour before searing them in a pan.

SCRAPPLE

1. Put the trotters, liver, and heart in a pot, and cover them with water. Boil the water over medium heat for ten minutes. After the scum (just denatured proteins), has risen to the top, dump the water and refill. Boil until the flesh of the meat is soft and falling off the bones, 2-4 hours. Check the pot every half hour, and remove any further scum that rises to the top with a spoon.

2. Remove the pot from the heat, and skim any remaining scum off the top of the broth.

3. Strain the broth, saving and setting aside the cooking liquid for later. Let the cooked meat cool enough to handle. Separate any remaining meat from the bones, and combine all of the meat in a grinder or food processor. Grind to a ground meat consistency, and set aside.

4. In the bowl of your food processor, combine 1½ quarts of still warm broth with the tapioca, arrowroot, and almond flours. Process until smooth, and then pulse in the ground meat.

5. Transfer the mixture to a clean pot, and simmer over medium heat for 30 minutes. Once reduced and thickened, add the salt, pepper, marjoram, mace, onion powder, and gelatin. Stir to combine.

6. Line 3 loaf pans with parchment or wax paper, and transfer the scrapple to the loaf pans. Refrigerate for 4-8 hours (overnight is ideal) until the loaves are firm.

7. To cook, slice the loaves into ½-inch slices.

8. Pour the additional almond flour (1-2 tablespoons per slice) into a shallow bowl, and dredge each side of the chilled scrapple in the almond flour.

9. Melt the Lard in a large skillet over medium-high heat.

10. Sear the scrapple slices for about 60 seconds per side; you want to sear for a nice brown color. Do not overcook, or the gelatinous scrapple might melt.

Who doesn't have fond childhood memories of *breakfast sausage?* Our version of the classic takes them to a whole new, healthier place. Serve them with our *Bacon Pumpkin Pancakes* (page 262). If stuffing sausages isn't your thing, this recipe is just as tasty in patty form. You can also use the loose meat to make our *Sausage & Mushroom Gravy* (page 254).

DIFFICULTY
Intermediate

TIME to TABLE
Under 30 minutes

YIELD
Makes 6 sausages

EQUIPMENT
Sausage stuffer

INGREDIENTS

1 pound ground pork

3 tablespoons maple syrup

2 teaspoons fresh sage, minced

1 teaspoon garlic powder

1 teaspoon salt

1 teaspoon fennel seed, ground

½ teaspoon ground coriander

¼ teaspoon pepper

Hot casings

Note: The key to cooking sausages all the way through is low and slow—as in, don't try to rush it with high heat. The larger the sausage, the longer it will need to cook.

Here's how to tell if a sausage is done: touch the center of it with your finger; if the meat feels firm without much give, it's ready. Do not "test" by cutting the sausage open with a knife—you'll lose all the delicious juices!

MAPLE SAGE BREAKFAST SAUSAGE LINKS

1. Combine all ingredients by hand. Set aside, and allow the flavors to combine for 5-10 minutes.

2. Using the sausage stuffing method described on page 58 to make sausage links, fill the hog casings. We suggest that each link be 1-inch wide and 4 inches long, but feel free to adjust the size to your taste.

3. Place the links in a cast-iron skillet, and cook them on medium-low heat for 10 minutes per side.

4. If the sausage links are not seared by the time they are cooked through, briefly turn up the heat.

DIFFICULTY
Basic

TIME TO TABLE
Less than 30 minutes

YEILD
About 8 patties

EQUIPMENT
Spice or coffee grinder or mortar and pestle

INGREDIENTS

1 tablespoon star anise points (about 5 or 6)

1 teaspoon salt

½ teaspoon whole cloves

½ teaspoon dried thyme

¼ teaspoon coriander

¼ teaspoon garlic powder

¼ teaspoon white pepper

¼ cup ice water

1 pound ground pork

Note: If you want to turn this recipe into sausage links, refer to instructions for sausage stuffing on page 58. The ingredients will make about eight 2-ounce sausages.

We try to have a *romantic weekend* away every couple of months. On one such weekend, at the Stone Manor Bed and Breakfast, we woke up to the *amazing smell of these sausages*, which the innkeepers had procured from a local farm. After eating more than our share, we knew we had to replicate the recipe—and that was before we even knew how to make sausages! In some ways, this is the recipe that *started it all*.

LICORICE SAUSAGE

1. In a spice or coffee grinder, or using a mortar and pestle, grind the star anise, salt, cloves, thyme, coriander, garlic powder, and white pepper into a fine powder.

2. Place the ice water in a large bowl, and add the spice mixture. Stir, and set aside for 15 minutes.

3. Add the pork to the wet spice mixture, and combine by hand (remove any remaining ice).

4. Set the mixture aside, and allow flavors to combine for 5-10 minutes.

5. Form the meat into patties of about 3 inches in diameter.

6. Cook over medium heat in a large skillet for about 4 minutes per side or until the patties are cooked through, with a crisp edge.

If Matt so much as smells sausage, he runs for the mustard and sauerkraut. One of his favorite dishes is thick Italian sausage served over *sautéed sweet bell peppers and caramelized onions*. Unfortunately, most store-bought sausages are made with low-quality pork and scary fillers, so naturally we had to figure out how to make them from scratch! Just be prepared: once the delectable aroma of Italian sausages fills the air, neighbors might show up.

DIFFICULTY
Intermediate

TIME TO TABLE
30-60 minutes

SERVES
2-4

EQUIPMENT
Meat grinder and sausage stuffer or food processor

INGREDIENTS
1 pound ground pork
¼ cup red wine
1 teaspoon salt
1 teaspoon dried parsley
1 teaspoon dried oregano
½ teaspoon dried basil
½ teaspoon red pepper flakes
¼ teaspoon white pepper
Hog casings

ITALIAN SAUSAGE LINKS

1. Combine all ingredients by hand. Set aside, and allow the flavors to combine for 5-10 minutes.

2. Using the method described for stuffing sausages on page 58, fill the hog casings and form the meat into links. We suggest sausages of 1 inch wide and 6 inches long.

3. In a cast-iron skillet, cook the sausages over medium-low heat for 10 minutes per side or until cooked through. (To determine if the sausages are done, refer to the finger test on page 78.)

4. If the links do not have a sear on the outside by the time they are cooked through, briefly turn up the heat.

5. We recommend caramelizing some sliced peppers and onions in the pan drippings once the sausage is removed.

Note: This recipe also works as patties; just fry them up in a skillet. Or use the loose meat to make our Pork Stuffing Casserole (page 240) or Porktastic Frittata (page 152).

You can't help but fall in love with the magical chorizo—from the unique spiciness, to that subtle vinegar tang, to the way it seems to *complement everything you pair it with.* We love these Mexican sausages with scrambled eggs or as part of our *Southwestern Chorizo Burgers* (page 108).

MEXICAN CHORIZO

1. Microwave the chilies for 20 seconds to soften. (You can also seal them in a bag and run them under hot water.)

2. Cut open each chili and remove the seeds and stem. Then, roughly chop them. Always wash your hands after touching hot peppers; the oils can irritate your skin and eyes!

3. Place the chilies, onion, and garlic in a bowl, and cover them with the apple cider vinegar.

4. Place a weight—another bowl with canned goods in it—on top of the covered bowl, and set it aside for 3 hours or longer.

5. In a food processor, pulse the wet pepper mixture along with the cumin, salt, pepper, and cinnamon until smooth.

6. With a spoon or gloved hands, thoroughly combine the ground pork with the pepper mixture. Chill until ready to use.

7. To serve, either stuff the pork into hog casings using the instructions on page 58, or use it loose in ground meat recipes or with scrambled eggs. Simply brown your chorizo over medium heat before adding the eggs.

DIFFICULTY
Intermediate

TIME TO TABLE
3-6 hours

SERVES
6-8

EQUIPMENT
Food processor

INGREDIENTS
5 dried chilies de arbol (red chili)

5 dried chipotle chilies

1 yellow onion, chopped

5 cloves garlic, minced

½ cup apple cider vinegar

1 tablespoon ground cumin

1 tablespoon salt

1 teaspoon pepper

¼ teaspoon cinnamon

2 pounds ground pork

Note: **We get our dried chilies at the local Asian food market, but you can also find them online.**

For detailed instructions on how to make and stuff this recipe into your own sausage links, refer to page 58.

If you don't live in an area with good Polish restaurants, we'll bet you haven't tasted *authentic* kielbasa. If the closest you've come are the bland, rubbery, vacuum-packed grocery store versions, then we're particularly excited about sharing this *culinary gem*—a traditional and beloved dish in Stacy's family. Try our *Kielbasa with Sauerkraut* (page 124), or serve it over *Mashed Cauliflower* (page 208). We're pretty sure it will become one of your favorites, too.

DIFFICULTY
Intermediate

TIME TO TABLE
Under 30 minutes

SERVES
6-8

EQUIPMENT
Sausage stuffer

INGREDIENTS

2 pounds ground pork

2 teaspoons salt

2 teaspoons fresh marjoram, finely chopped

1 teaspoon sweet Hungarian paprika

1 teaspoon dry mustard

½ teaspoon garlic powder

½ teaspoon black pepper

½ cup cold water

Hog casings

KIELBASA

1. Combine all ingredients by hand. Set it aside, and allow the flavors to combine for 5-10 minutes.

2. Using the method described for stuffing sausages on page 58, fill the hog casings and form the meat into links. We suggest long sausages of at least 12 inches if making Kielbasa with Sauerkraut (page 124) or 6 inches otherwise.

3. In a cast-iron skillet, cook the sausages on medium-low heat for 10 minutes per side or until cooked through. (To determine if the sausages are done, refer to the finger test on page 78.)

4. Alternatively, cook the sausages using the recipe for Kielbasa with Sauerkraut on page 124, or cook on low for 8 hours in a slow cooker with cabbage and Pork Stock.

Note: **For detailed instructions on how to make and stuff your own sausage links, refer to the How To section, page 58.**

Humans have been using smoke to cook and preserve food almost since the invention of cooking itself. In fact, you could say the fire pit was the world's first crockpot! People around the world have been using various kinds of wood to imbue their meat with delicious, smoky flavors for thousands of years. Perhaps the most famous of these is Hawaii's "Kalua Pig," which involves burying a whole animal in the ground with hardwoods and charcoals.

Don't worry; it doesn't require that much effort to give your food a smoky taste. Follow the instructions on page 54 and you'll be smoking in no time. Just be sure to make enough for the neighbors—the aromas are pretty irresistible!

PLAY WITH FIRE: Grilled & Smoked Recipes

DIFFICULTY
Basic

TIME to TABLE
6-12 hours

SERVES
4-6

PREHEAT
Grill to medium-high

EQUIPMENT
Skewers (bamboo, or metal); grill

INGREDIENTS

¼ cup coconut aminos or wheat-free tamari

1 garlic clove, minced

1 teaspoon chili powder

1 teaspoon ground cumin

1 teaspoon sweet Hungarian paprika

½ teaspoon salt

¼ teaspoon ground cloves

2 pounds pork shoulder, trimmed and cut into 1-inch cubes

1 yellow onion, cut into 8 sections

1 green bell pepper, cut into 1-inch squares

1 red bell pepper, cut into 1-inch squares

1 pineapple, cut into 1-inch cubes

If you're as sick as we are of the dried-out grilled chicken that's become a staple at *summer barbecues*, then you're in luck. One of our most popular party menus is *Make Your Own Kabobs*. We set up ingredients in bowls and let people skewer their own *preferred meat and veggies*. Our preference, of course, are kabobs made from pork shoulder; the slightly fattier cut produces the moistest and most incredibly flavorful kabobs you will ever eat. It also provides the perfect complement to the *sweet, caramelized vegetables and fruit.*

GRILLED CUBED PORK KABOBS

1. In a medium-sized mixing bowl, whisk together the coconut aminos, garlic, chili powder, cumin, Hungarian paprika, salt, and cloves.

2. Stir in the meat, coating it with the spice mixture. Then, cover the bowl, and refrigerate it for 6-12 hours.

3. If using bamboo skewers, soak them in water for 30 minutes before loading. This will help prevent the wood from catching fire.

4. Place the meat and vegetables on the skewers. We recommend flanking each piece of meat with pineapple or veggies so that each can absorb some of the pork fat.

5. Grill the kabobs over medium-high heat with the lid closed for 6-10 minutes or until the pork is cooked through. You can check the internal temperature with a meat thermometer; 150-170°F is ideal, depending on your preference of medium or well done.

6. Serve the kabobs on the skewers, or remove the meat and veggies from the skewers and serve them in a bowl over Turnip and Parsnip Purée (page 224).

DIFFICULTY
Intermediate

TIME to TABLE
6-12 hours

SERVES
8-10

PREHEAT
Smoldering coals to 225°F.

EQUIPMENT
Smoker or alternate set-up (page 54)

INGREDIENTS

5 pounds pork shoulder

1 tablespoon salt

1 tablespoon maple, date, or palm granulated sugar

2 teaspoons sweet Hungarian paprika

1 teaspoon black pepper

1 teaspoon lemon zest

½ teaspoon ground mustard

¼ teaspoon cayenne pepper

Pulled pork is, *in our opinion*, the most delicious meat dish you can serve, as long as you do it right. A *perfectly prepared pulled pork shoulder* has a pinkish purple ring under the skin, a crispy outer skin, and moist meat that shreds easily. We recommend a Boston butt cut (it's not actually the pig's behind, that's the ham), but a picnic shoulder will do just as well. Pulled pork might seem like an overwhelmingly difficult dish to prepare, but it's not as hard as you think, and the *payoff in taste* is definitely worth the effort, especially when paired with homemade barbecue sauces (pages 248 and 250).

SMOKED PULLED PORK SHOULDER

1. Dry the outside of the meat with a towel.

2. In a small bowl, make the rub by combining the salt, sugar, Hungarian paprika, black pepper, lemon zest, mustard, and cayenne pepper.

3. Pat the outside of the meat with the rub until it is completely covered.

4. Smoke the meat at 225°F for 6 hours (or about 1 hour more than the number of pounds of meat), per the instructions on page 54, until it shreds easily and completely. To ensure that you do not overcook the pork, test the meat every hour or so by gently pulling it with a fork to see if the middle of the flesh releases easily. When the center becomes tender but is not quite ready, check more frequently to prevent the meat from drying out. The final internal temperature should be 185°F.

5. Let the pork shoulder rest for 10-20 minutes before shredding the meat and serving. Be prepared: who gets the crispy skin can lead to fist fights!

The ideal burger ought to be thick and juicy, but can it also be refreshing? Sure! Infusing the meat with bright and acidic citrus flavors adds a *lighter taste* without taking anything away from everything you already *love about burgers.*

For those who eat local and seasonally, this is a great *winter option* if you're sick of heavy root vegetables. You can pretty much always find citrus. This also happens to be *one of our most requested recipes,* and it works just as well for meatballs.

DIFFICULTY
Basic

TIME TO TABLE
Under 30 minutes

SERVES
4-6

PREHEAT
Grill to high

EQUIPMENT
Grill or grill pan

INGREDIENTS

2 pounds ground pork

1 tablespoon orange juice, freshly squeezed

1 tablespoon lemon juice, freshly squeezed

1 tablespoon fresh mint, chopped

1 teaspoon lemon zest

1 teaspoon orange zest

1 garlic clove, minced

½ teaspoon salt

⅛ teaspoon pepper

Note: To transform this recipe into an on-the-go snack or party favorite, form tablespoon-sized meatballs and bake at 350°F for 20 minutes, or until cooked through.

CITRUS INFUSED PORK BURGERS

1. Thoroughly combine all ingredients.

2. Allow the meat to rest for 30 minutes. Try to handle the meat as little as possible, which helps to keep it tender and loose.

3. Form the meat into 6 patties of about 4 inches in diameter—a little wider than a beef patty (pork is higher in fat and, therefore, shrinks as it cooks). Be gentle with your patties; try to keep them as loose as you can while still maintaining their shape. A compact burger will dry out and have a coarser texture.

4. Grill the patties over high heat, about 8 minutes per side. Check the burgers by touching the center. It should be stiff but still have some give. You don't want a medium-rare burger; internal temperature should reach about 160°F.

5. To retain moisture, let the burgers rest for a few minutes before serving. We like to serve them in Boston bibb lettuce cups topped with a fresh orange segment and a mint leaf or with our Sweet Potato Drop Biscuits (page 222).

When Matt pulled our first smoked pork belly off the grill, Stacy and Aimee (our photographer) were initially put off by the gnarly-looking, charred piece of meat. The *rich and delicious fat* of the pastured pork had caused the meat to catch fire in the smoker, and we weren't even sure if it was edible. But as we cut in and found the tender, juicy, delicious meat, Stacy said, *"If this is how good smoked belly tastes, I don't ever want to eat bacon again!"* Seriously, we can't recommend this recipe enough—it has become one of our absolute favorites.

DIFFICULTY
Intermediate

TIME to TABLE
3 hours

SERVES
4-6

PREHEAT
Smoldering coals need to reach 225°F

EQUIPMENT
Smoker or alternate set-up (page 54)

INGREDIENTS

3 pounds pork belly

1 tablespoon salt

1 teaspoon ground coriander

1 teaspoon ground cumin

1 teaspoon ground cardamom

1 teaspoon garlic powder

½ teaspoon lemon zest

¼ teaspoon black pepper

SMOKED PORK BELLY

1. Dry the outside of the pork belly with a towel.

2. In a small bowl, make the rub by combining the salt, coriander, cumin, cardamom, garlic powder, lemon zest, and black pepper.

3. Rub the outside of the meat with the spices until it is completely covered.

4. Place the meat into the smoker, ensuring that the coals have died down to a smolder and a temperature of 225°F. Pork belly is such a fatty cut of meat it may catch fire, but that's okay! Any charring will add great flavor to the meat. Just check on it every 20-30 minutes, and put the flames out if/when they appear.

5. Smoke the meat for about 3 hours until it is cooked through. The pork should reach an internal temperature of 175-180°F. The meat should have some give and tenderness when you touch it. Don't let it get firm or it will be overcooked!

DIFFICULTY
Basic

TIME ṯo TABLE
30-60 minutes

SERVES
4-6

PREHEAT
Grill to medium

EQUIPMENT
Grill

INGREDIENTS

2 pounds pork tenderloin

1 teaspoon ground cumin

1 teaspoon salt

½ teaspoon black pepper

½ teaspoon chili powder

½ teaspoon ground allspice

½ teaspoon ground ginger

½ teaspoon sweet Hungarian
  paprika

⅛-½ teaspoon cayenne
  pepper

¼ teaspoon cinnamon

⅛ teaspoon white pepper

**Note: If you'd like
to cook inside, we
recommend baking in
the oven at 350°F for
30-40 minutes.**

If the idea of the most tender part of the pig *crusted with spices* and grilled to perfection doesn't get you excited, we don't know what more we can do for you! The tenderloin is just what it sounds like: an incredibly lean yet tender piece of meat. We've created *a simple, not-too-spicy rub* that forms into a delicious crust. It pairs brilliantly with a simple fresh salad and *Mashed Cauliflower* (page 208). Just be careful not to overcook it or you'll lose the tenderness; medium-rare is optimal.

CAJUN RUBBED TENDERLOIN

1. Pat the pork tenderloin dry with a towel.

2. In a small bowl, make the rub by combining the cumin, salt, black pepper, chili powder, allspice, ginger, Hungarian paprika, cayenne pepper, cinnamon, and white pepper. Mix spices into a rub.

3. Coat the tenderloin with the spices until it is completely covered.

4. Grill the meat on medium heat for about 15 minutes per side or until the internal temperature reaches about 140°F. Remove the meat from the heat, cover it with a foil tent to retain heat and moisture, and let it rest for 10 minutes or until the internal temperature rises to about 145°F. The inside will still be slightly pink and tender when fully cooked.

In our first book, *Eat Like a Dinosaur*, one of the most beloved recipes was 50/50 Burgers—that's *50 percent* pork bacon, and *50 percent* ground beef. We'd had a similar dish in a restaurant, and we made it our own. In this update, we use ground pork instead of pork bacon. (You should have plenty of ground pork lying around if you've bought a whole hog from your local farmer!) To get the original's same bacon-beefy flavor, we subbed beef bacon for the ground beef. *The result?* Another uniquely smoky burger!

Serve with Sriracha (a hot chili sauce), guacamole, or mustard and sauerkraut. Our *Faux-Tato Salad* (page 212), is a great side.

DIFFICULTY
Basic

TIME to TABLE
Under 30 minutes

SERVES
4-6

PREHEAT
Grill or flame to medium-high heat

EQUIPMENT
Meat grinder or food processor; grill or grill pan

INGREDIENTS
1 pound beef bacon

1 pound ground pork

1 teaspoon salt

1 teaspoon chili powder

½ teaspoon ground cumin

¼ teaspoon black pepper

50/50 BURGERS, TAKE 2

1. Using a meat grinder or food processor with a blade attachment, process the beef bacon until it is a similar consistency as the ground pork.

2. Mix the meats, salt, chili powder, cumin, and black pepper by hand in a large bowl.

3. Form the meat into 6 patties of about 4 inches in diameter—a little wider than a beef patty (pork is higher in fat and, therefore, shrinks as it cooks). Be gentle with your patties; try to keep them as loose as you can while still maintaining their shape. A compact burger will dry out and have a coarser texture.

4. Grill the patties over high heat for about 10 minutes per side. You don't want a medium rare burger; the internal temperature should reach about 160°F.

5. To retain moisture, let the meat rest for a few minutes before serving.

DIFFICULTY
Basic

TIME to TABLE
1-2 hours

SERVES
4-6

PREHEAT
Grill to medium-low

EQUIPMENT
Grill

INGREDIENTS

4 pounds pork backbone, butchered into individual pieces

1 tablespoon date, palm, or maple granulated sugar

1 tablespoon sea salt

2 teaspoons sweet Hungarian paprika

1 teaspoon garlic powder

1 teaspoon black pepper

1 teaspoon lemon zest

½ teaspoon ground turmeric

Note: If you want to cook these inside, we recommend oven roasting at 325°F for 90 minutes. Finishing over fire does add that extra flavor you'll want!

One of the first cuts of meat we purchased from Polyface Farms was backbone. We were told by the shop attendant that this cut is *incredibly juicy and tender,* but not overwhelmingly popular and therefore pretty affordable. We've been exploiting its unpopularity ever since!

Backbone is the meaty back area of the pig's ribs, so be aware that this cut won't be an option if you choose bone-in rib chops when processing your whole hog. Backbone is often called *Country Style,* particularly in supermarkets. Whatever you call it, there's so much tender meat with each delicious piece it *rivals a T-bone steak.* We suggest you pair these ribs with our *BBQ Sauce, Texas Style* (page 250). Be careful: you just may fall in love.

PICNIC RIBS |BACKBONE|

1. Pat each piece of meat dry with a towel.

2. In a small bowl, make the rub by combining the sugar, salt, Hungarian paprika, garlic powder, black pepper, lemon zest, and turmeric.

3. Rub all surfaces of each piece of meat with the spice mixture.

4. Wrap the backbones in aluminum foil, sealing tight, and place them on the center of the preheated grill over medium-low heat. Grill for 75 minutes.

5. Remove the meat from the heat, and allow it to rest for 5 minutes before carefully removing it from the foil.

6. Turn up the grill to medium-high heat while the meat is resting, and finish the meat by searing it over the heat for 1-2 minutes on each side.

The Paleo lifestyle isn't very Asian food-friendly thanks to the soy, vegetable oils, and gluten hiding in the sauces. It is best to stay away from Asian food unless you are *creating dishes like this at home.* We love these ribs with our *Sautéed Green Beans* (page 216) and *Pork Fried Cauliflower Rice* (page 206).

DIFFICULTY
Intermediate

TIME to TABLE
6-12 hours

SERVES
4-6

PREHEAT
Grill to medium-high

EQUIPMENT
Grill; pastry brush

INGREDIENTS

MARINADE:

¾ cup Pork Stock (page 66)

¼ cup coconut aminos or wheat-free tamari

2 teaspoons ginger, fresh or ground (fresh preferred)

2 teaspoons sesame oil

2 teaspoons fish sauce (Red Boat brand recommended)

3 cloves garlic, minced

¼ cup apple cider vinegar

1 dried chili (red chili or chili de arbol preferred), seeds removed and diced

¼ cup honey

¼ teaspoon white pepper

3 pounds pork short ribs, also known as rib tips

SAUCE:

½ cup coconut aminos or wheat-free tamari

½ cup blackstrap molasses

⅓ cup tahini

1 teaspoon fish sauce (Red Boat brand recommended)

ASIAN SHORT RIBS

1. In a small saucepan, whisk together the Pork Stock, coconut aminos, ginger, sesame oil, fish sauce, garlic, apple cider vinegar, chili, honey, and white pepper for the marinade.

2. Warm the marinade on the stovetop for a few minutes to activate and combine the flavors. Remove the marinade from the heat, and let it cool for at least 10 minutes.

3. Place the short ribs in a large airtight container, and pour the cooled marinade over the ribs until they are covered. Refrigerate for at least 8 hours (overnight is best).

4. When you're ready to cook the ribs, first prepare the sauce by whisking the coconut aminos, molasses, tahini, and fish sauce together. It's fine if the sauce is slightly chunky; the ingredients will melt together as the ribs cook. Set aside a portion of the sauce to serve with the ribs.

5. Remove the ribs from the marinade, and place them on a plate, letting the excess liquid drip off before spreading the sauce on each rib with a pastry brush. Make sure all sides are coated thickly and evenly.

6. Grill the meat over medium-high heat for about 8 minutes on each side, brushing the sauce on it again after turning it and after removing it from the grill. Leave the grill open to watch and prevent flare-ups. Short ribs don't need to cook long, as they are a relatively tender cut (compared to spare ribs, for example), and the acidic marinade will help to tenderize the meat before it's cooked. Make sure the ribs are cooked through to about 155°F on the grill, however.

7. Once cooked through, remove the ribs from the heat, cover them for about 10 minutes to let them rest and finish cooking to 160°F internally. Serve the ribs with the remaining sauce.

DIFFICULTY
Intermediate

TIME TO TABLE
6-12 hours

SERVES
4-6 (each rack serves 2-3 people)

PREHEAT
Smoldering coals to 225°F

EQUIPMENT
Smoker or alternate set-up (see page 54)

INGREDIENTS

2 racks pork spare ribs, about 4 pounds

¼ cup maple, date, or palm granulated sugar

1 tablespoon chili powder

1 tablespoon ground cumin

2 teaspoons salt

2 teaspoons dry mustard

1 teaspoon garlic powder

1 teaspoon onion powder

½ teaspoon white pepper

½ teaspoon cayenne pepper

When people think about barbecuing pork, *this is the dish they think of.* But despite their ubiquity, smoked spare ribs —like pulled pork— *are hard to get right.* We've taste-tested them all over the United States. What we've found is that, more often than not, the ribs delivered to our table are dry and flavorless — which is why they are served with a bucket of sugary syrup!

When we do find good ribs, they're usually at some *tiny roadside stand,* where they've been smoked all day; the taste is so powerfully flavorful, you don't even need sauce!

This recipe will help you recreate that *authentic barbecue flavor in your own backyard.* Keep in mind that there are people who spend a lifetime getting smoked ribs just right, so give yourself some time to perfect them.

SMOKED SPARE RIBS

1. Let the ribs rest at room temperature for at least 30 minutes. Then, pat the outside of the meat dry with a towel.

2. In a small bowl, make the rub by combining the sugar, chili powder, cumin, salt, mustard, garlic powder, onion powder, white pepper, and cayenne pepper with a fork.

3. Pat the outside of the meat with the rub until it is completely covered.

4. Following the instructions on page 54, smoke the ribs at 225°F for 5 hours (about 1 hour more than the number of pounds of meat). Keep the coals smoldering at low heat so that the ribs don't burn, catch fire, or overcook (check periodically to make sure they aren't drying out.) Flip and move the ribs 90 degrees every hour in order to get cross-hatch sear marks across the flesh. The meat is cooked when it is tender and easily releases from the bone.

5. Remove the ribs from the heat, and let them rest uncovered for 10 minutes before serving. If you want to add BBQ sauce, we recommend our Carolina Style (page 248).

After having this *spicy, juicy, boldly-flavored burger* with a runny egg on top, you may have a new favorite breakfast dish—especially if you make the *Chorizo from scratch* (page 84). The creamy egg yolks and a bit of guacamole perfectly cool the chorizo's spicy, intense flavor.

DIFFICULTY
Basic

TIME TO TABLE
Under 30 minutes

SERVES
4-6

PREHEAT
Grill to medium

EQUIPMENT
Grill or grill pan

INGREDIENTS

1 pound ground pork

1 pound Mexican Chorizo (page 84)

4 tablespoons bacon fat or Lard (page 62), divided

6 eggs

Butter lettuce leaves (optional)

Guacamole (optional)

SOUTHWESTERN CHORIZO BURGERS WITH FRIED EGGS

1. Mix the meats by hand in a large bowl.

2. Form the meat mixture into 6 patties of about 4 inches in diameter—a little wider than a beef patty (pork is higher in fat and, therefore, shrinks as it cooks). Be gentle with your patties; try to keep them as loose as you can while still maintaining their shape. A compact burger will dry out and have a coarser texture.

3. Grill the patties over high heat for about 10 minutes per side. Check the burgers by touching the center; it should be firm with some give. You don't want a medium rare burger, so the internal temperature should be about 160°F.

4. Meanwhile, melt one tablespoon of bacon fat in a frying pan (stainless steel recommended) over medium-low heat. Crack an egg into the pan, and cover it. Cooking at a lower temperature will allow the egg white to cook all the way through while still leaving the yolk runny. Watch closely; as soon as the white becomes fully opaque, remove the egg from the pan.

5. Fry each egg in this manner, adding an extra tablespoon of fat when the pan goes dry.

6. To serve, build your burger with the lettuce acting as the bottom of your bun, and top the burger with the egg and guacamole.

If you've followed our instructions for making our Pork Stock on page 66, you now have quarts of delicious liquid gold lying around. Allow us to show you how to use it!

Consuming rich pork stock will add lots of nutritional value to your diet. It's high in trace minerals like calcium, magnesium, and phosphorous, and packed with gelatin and collagen, which facilitate health and good digestion. You know how your stock solidified into a soft, jiggling mass that Bill Cosby would love? That's the gelatin at work and it means you made something terrific!

SOUPS & STEWS

We sometimes call this *"breakfast soup"* since we often make a big batch on the weekend and our kids eat it in the morning before school. Soup might not be a traditional breakfast food in the West, as it is in Asia, but it's actually the most nourishing way to *start your day*—particularly when it's made with pastured, nutrient-dense eggs and homemade Pork Stock (page 66). Believe it or not, our boys love it!

DIFFICULTY
Basic

TIME to TABLE
Less than 30 minutes

SERVES
4-6

INGREDIENTS

2 tablespoons Lard (page 62)

1 yellow onion, diced

4 cups Pork Stock (page 66)

1 teaspoon fish sauce (Red Boat brand recommended)

1 teaspoon sesame oil

½ teaspoon ginger, fresh or ground (fresh preferred)

2 tablespoons arrowroot powder

2 tablespoons water

4 eggs, scrambled

EGG DROP SOUP

1. In a large stockpot, melt the Lard over medium-high heat.

2. Sauté the onion until soft, stirring occasionally.

3. Add the Pork Stock, fish sauce, sesame oil, and ginger, and turn the heat to high.

4. In a small bowl, prepare a slurry by mixing together the arrowroot powder and water until smooth.

5. When the stock boils, add the slurry, and whisk together well.

6. Slowly drizzle thin ribbons of the uncooked scrambled eggs into the boiling stock. They will immediately cook into thin strands.

7. Remove the pot from the heat, and serve. If storing in the fridge, let the soup cool slightly first. This soup freezes well in individual airtight containers; just thaw it in the fridge before reheating.

DIFFICULTY
Basic

TIME to TABLE
Less than 4 hours

SERVES
6-8

INGREDIENTS

2 tablespoons Lard (page 62)

1 onion, ½-inch dice

2 carrots, ½-inch dice

2 parsnips, ½-inch dice

4 golden beets, ½-inch dice

2 cloves garlic, minced

1 meaty ham bone, about 2 pounds

2 bay leaves

1 teaspoon fresh sage, chopped

1 teaspoon fresh tarragon, chopped

½ teaspoon salt

¼ teaspoon white pepper

6 cups Pork Stock (page 66)

Growing up, there used to be a prepared bag of beans and seasonings sold in the grocery store: *Ham Bone Soup Mix*. It was somewhat magical, soaking these hard-as-a-rock beans in water overnight and ending up with a soft bean soup the next evening. *Nostalgic for this classic dish,* we set out to recreate a bean soup without beans. It is actually much simpler and, perhaps, even more nourishing and satisfying—not to mention there's no digestive distress!

Serve the soup with *Homestyle Biscuits* (page 218) and *Lard Butter* (page 246).

HAM BONE SOUP

1. In a large stockpot, melt the Lard over medium heat.

2. Add the onion, carrots, parsnips, beets, and garlic, and sauté until soft, about 7 minutes, stirring occasionally.

3. Add the ham bone, bay leaves, sage, tarragon, salt, white pepper, and Pork Stock, and bring the soup to a boil over high heat.

4. Reduce the heat to low, and cover. Simmer for about 3 hours, until the remaining meat from the ham is falling off of the bone.

5. Shred the remaining meat into the soup, remove the bone and bay leaves, and serve.

DIFFICULTY
Advanced

TIME to TABLE
More than 24 hours

SERVES
6-8

EQUIPMENT
Stockpot

INGREDIENTS

2 pounds chitterlings, cleaned

48 ounces Pork Stock (page 66)

5 star anise pods

5 allspice berries

3 whole cloves

1 slice dried ginger, ⅛ inch thick

2 pounds ground pork

GARNISH FOR
EACH BOWL:

1 yellow onion, sliced

1 green onion, sliced

1 tablespoon fish sauce (Red Boat brand preferred)

¼ cup broccoli or alfalfa sprouts

1 jalapeno, sliced

10 Thai basil leaves

1 tablespoon fresh cilantro or mint, chopped

½ lime, cut into wedges

Note: **If you want to make pho without the chitterlings? Perhaps try the zucchini noodles we make on page 234.**

There is no way around the fact that chitterlings — the small intestines of pigs — are not appetizing to a lot of people. Nor are they the most pleasant food to cook. But if you prepare and serve them right, they become the perfect replacement for rice noodles (they are similar in texture), with the added bonus of the *super minerals selenium, zinc, copper, and iron!*

When you buy chitterlings, be sure they are cleaned or marked "prepared." We recommend you boil the chitterlings a day before you make the pho; the smell is pungent and can permeate your house. However, the guests we've served this to find the dish to be *delicious,* so it was worth the stink.

PHO WITH CHITTERLING NOODLES

1. Cut the chitterlings into 6-inch lengths, and rinse them in fresh water several times. Cover them with water and a tablespoon of salt in an airtight container, and store in the refrigerator overnight.

2. The next day, in a large pot, boil the chitterlings in clean, salted water for 2 hours.

3. Drain the pot, rinse the chitterlings thoroughly with fresh water, and allow them to cool. Once cooled, open each piece, and scrape the fat from the inside to remove any pungent smell. Also remove any fatty nodules, but do not worry about creating holes.

4. Slice the chitterlings into ¼-inch thick ribbons that resemble noodles.

5. In a new, clean pot, combine the Pork Stock, anise pods, allspice berries, whole cloves, ginger, and "noodles," and bring the liquid to a boil.

6. Once boiling, reduce the heat to low, and simmer for 2 hours.

7. Ten minutes before serving, form the ground pork into 1-inch balls, and allow them to cook in the broth. No spices are needed, as the broth will flavor the meat.

8. Remove the pot from the heat, and serve the soup with any or all of the garnishes to taste.

DIFFICULTY
Basic

TIME to TABLE
30-60 minutes

SERVES
4-6

EQUIPMENT
Immersion blender or blender

INGREDIENTS

1 acorn squash, peeled, seeds removed, and cut into 1-inch chunks

3 tablespoons Lard (page 62), divided

1 yellow onion, diced

1 clove garlic, minced

2 cups Pork Stock (page 66)

1 teaspoon sweet Hungarian paprika

½ teaspoon salt

¼ teaspoon ground nutmeg

⅛ teaspoon ground cloves

¼ teaspoon black pepper

¼ cup Crispy Lardons (page 190), warmed

Acorn squash is the neglected cousin of butternut squash and pumpkin. The latter two have a *sweeter taste*, but acorn squash has its own merits and deserves its day on the stove. After making versions of this creamy soup for years, we've come to appreciate the *"green pumpkin."*

If you don't have crispy lardons, anything *crispy* can be used as a replacement topping: crumbled bacon, pork rinds, or even toasted walnuts. If you are feeling *very* brave, try crispy roasted snout, a *unique treat!* Just roast at a high temperature and thinly slice on top of the finished soup.

ACORN SQUASH SOUP
with CRISPY LARDONS

1. Toss the acorn squash chunks with 1 tablespoon of Lard, and place them on a baking sheet.

2. Roast the squash at 350°F for 30 minutes, until it begins to caramelize and is soft enough to pierce with a fork.

3. In a medium-sized pot, melt the remaining 2 tablespoons of Lard over medium heat.

4. Add the onion and garlic, and sauté for about 5 minutes or until softened, stirring occasionally.

5. Add the squash and Pork Stock, and bring the soup to a boil over high heat.

6. Cover, and reduce the heat to low. Simmer for 20 minutes.

7. Stir in the Hungarian paprika, salt, nutmeg, cloves, and black pepper, and use an immersion blender to purée the soup. You can use a regular blender, but you'll have to purée it in batches, and be careful of the steam.

8. Sprinkle the warmed Crispy Lardons on top of the soup, and serve.

This bright red, *velvety soup* reminds us of the fairy tale *Snow White*, when the evil queen requests Snow White's heart from the huntsman and gets a pig's heart instead. Yes, there's a pig's heart in this stew! Don't be frightened: the heart and tongue are the mildest tasting of organ meats because they are muscles. And by stewing the heart in this acidic brew, the chewy meat becomes *deliciously tenderized*. For these reasons, Hunstman Stew is *an excellent introduction to offal*.

DIFFICULTY
Intermediate

TIME to TABLE
1-2 hours

SERVES
6-8

EQUIPMENT
Large stockpot

INGREDIENTS

1 tablespoon Lard (page 62)

1 pork heart, diced into ½-inch cubes

4 red beets, peeled and diced into ½-inch cubes

1 red onion, diced

1 carrot, diced into ½-inch cubes

2 cloves garlic, minced

2 tomatoes, diced into ½-inch cubes

½ cup dark red wine (drinking quality)

3 cups Pork Stock (page 66)

2 pork tails or 1 trotter or meaty soup bones

2 teaspoons fresh thyme

2 bay leaves

1 teaspoon salt

¼ teaspoon white pepper

HUNTSMAN STEW

1. In large stockpot, melt the Lard over medium heat.

2. Brown the heart pieces on all sides. Remove them to a plate, and set aside.

3. Add the beets, onion, carrot, and garlic to the pot, and sauté for 8 minutes.

4. Add the tomatoes, and bring to a simmer over medium-high heat.

5. Add the red wine, Pork Stock, tails, cooked heart, thyme, bay leaves, salt, and white pepper, and bring to a boil.

6. Reduce the heat to medium-low, and cover the pot. Simmer for 90 minutes or until the meat falls off of the tailbones.

7. Remove the bones and bay leaves before serving.

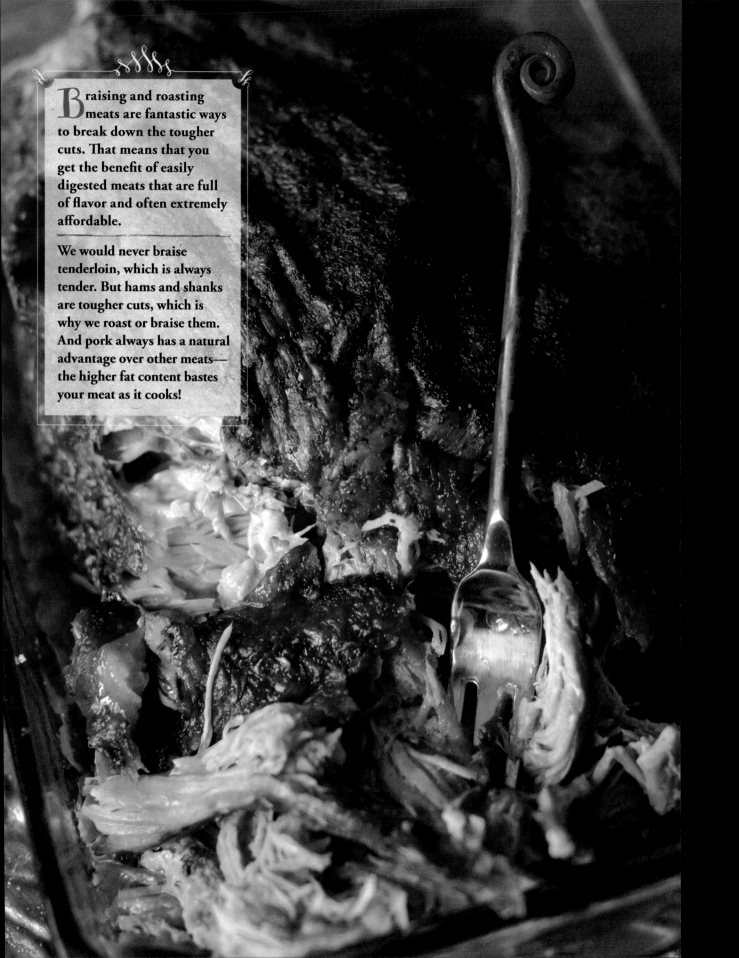

Braising and roasting meats are fantastic ways to break down the tougher cuts. That means that you get the benefit of easily digested meats that are full of flavor and often extremely affordable.

We would never braise tenderloin, which is always tender. But hams and shanks are tougher cuts, which is why we roast or braise them. And pork always has a natural advantage over other meats— the higher fat content bastes your meat as it cooks!

BRAISED AND ROASTED PORK

True fermented sauerkraut contains billions of beneficial microbes that, potentially, *improve your gut health* tremendously. With all that precious probiotic cargo, why would you cook it literally to death in the oven just to flavor your sausages? In our recipe, you get the flavors of kraut with simple ingredients, then serve the rest raw and alive, so you get the same *great taste* and all the *good nutrients!*

DIFFICULTY
Basic

TIME TO TABLE
Less than 90 minutes

SERVES
4-6

PREHEAT
Oven to 350°F

INGREDIENTS

2 pounds Kielbasa (page 86)

1 yellow onion, thinly sliced

2 green apples, cored, peeled, and grated

¼ cup raw sauerkraut, plus additional for serving

¼ cup apple cider vinegar

1 teaspoon sweet Hungarian paprika

KIELBASA WITH SAUERKRAUT

1. Lay the raw kielbasa sausage in a shallow baking dish.

2. In a medium bowl, combine the onion, apples, sauerkraut, apple cider vinegar, and Hungarian paprika until thoroughly mixed.

3. Pour the mixture on top of the kielbasa.

4. Cover, and bake at 350°F for 60 minutes.

5. Serve with additional raw sauerkraut and Mashed Cauliflower (page 208).

DIFFICULTY
Basic

TIME to TABLE
Less than 2 hours

SERVES
8-10

PREHEAT
Oven to 325°F

EQUIPMENT
Food processor

INGREDIENTS

5 pound ham leg, bone-in and spiral cut

1 cup mint leaves

6 garlic cloves

½ cup light olive oil

2 tablespoons sweet Hungarian paprika

2 tablespoons ground cumin

1 tablespoon black peppercorns

1 tablespoon cinnamon

2 teaspoons salt

1 teaspoon Garam Masala

½ teaspoon ground cloves

If you've ever had *the pleasure* of eating a leg of lamb meat gyro (where the spiced meat is roasted on a vertical spit), you'll understand the intention of this recipe. It evokes that *classic Greek flavor* without the weird fillers or the expensive leg of lamb. We highly recommend serving this with the *Avo-Ziki* sauce recipe found in *Practical Paleo* by Diane Sanfilippo, but a mint jelly or gluten-free yogurt-based dip will do just as well.

LAMB-STYLE LEG OF PIG

1. Ask your butcher to spiral cut your ham leg for you. It will make removal and cutting of the meat after cooking much easier.

2. Allow the leg of ham to come close to room temperature by setting it out for about 20 minutes.

3. While you wait, pat the outside of the ham leg dry with a towel.

4. In a food processor, pulse the mint leaves, garlic, olive oil, Hungarian paprika, cumin, peppercorns, cinnamon, salt, Garam Masala, and cloves into a thick paste.

5. Rub the outside of the entire leg with the spice mixture until it is thickly and evenly coated.

6. Roast the ham uncovered on a raised rack (so that the roast does not sit in the drippings) at 325°F for 90 minutes. The outside will be moist and bubbly, and the interior will be slightly pink and tender with an internal temperature of 145°F.

7. Serve the ham inside lettuce wraps with your preferred sauce or dip, fresh mint leaves, dill sprigs, and freshly chopped red onion.

Pot roast is the traditional, *go-to comfort food* for many families; its hearty beefiness is warming on a cool autumn evening. Not to mention, it's a very affordable cut of meat! Unfortunately, pot roasts can also be dry, bland, and unsatisfying. With this pork version, we've turned up the flavor and added a spicy horseradish mustard glaze to keep it *moist*. And the cabbage that cooks along with it will be infused with *more flavor* than any white potato ever would!

DIFFICULTY
Basic

TIME to TABLE
3-6 hours

SERVES
6-8

PREHEAT
Oven to 325°F

EQUIPMENT
Dutch oven

INGREDIENTS

¼ cup brown mustard

1 tablespoon maple, date, or palm granulated sugar

2 teaspoons prepared grated horseradish

1 teaspoon salt

½ teaspoon garlic powder

¼ teaspoon black pepper

5 pounds ham roast

1 cup apple cider (the cloudy kind made from real apples, NOT vinegar)

1 tablespoon Lard (page 62)

1 medium yellow onion, sliced in ¼ inch rounds

½ head cabbage, sliced into ¼-inch ribbons

HAM POT ROAST WITH HORSERADISH MUSTARD GLAZE

1. In a small bowl, mix the brown mustard, sugar, horseradish, salt, garlic powder, and black pepper into a paste with a fork.

2. Coat both sides of the roast with the paste.

3. Melt the Lard over medium heat in a Dutch oven. Brown each side of the roast, about 5 minutes per side.

4. Remove the roast from the pan, and pour in the apple cider, deglazing the bottom of the pan by gently scraping it to remove the remaining food bits.

5. Add the onion and cabbage to the pan, and place the roast on top of the veggies.

6. Cover the Dutch oven, and roast the veggies and meat for 3 hours at 325°F until the internal temperature reaches 160°F.

7. Serve with a root vegetable dish, like our Rosemary Carrot Mash (page 220) or Turnip & Parsnip Purée (page 224).

DIFFICULTY
Basic

TIME TO **TABLE**
1-2 hours

SERVES
4-6

PREHEAT
Oven to 325°F

INGREDIENTS

½ teaspoon salt

¼ teaspoon black pepper

3 pounds pork neck roast

1 yellow onion, sliced

2 cups Pork Stock (page 66)

1 tablespoon fresh sage, sliced

1 tablespoon fresh flat leaf Italian parsley, chopped

If pigs have no necks, then why is this neck roast so delicious? Don't be scared because this is a cut you haven't heard of. It's close in texture and flavor to the jowl of the pig, which is a *delicate and delicious* cut of meat—similar to bacon. *Impress your friends* with this succulent and unexpected dish. If you can't find neck roast, you can substitute any fatty muscle meat.

BRAISED NECK ROAST

1. Sprinkle salt and black pepper on each side of the neck roast.

2. Spread the onion slices on the bottom of a large cast-iron skillet, and place the roast on top.

3. Pour the Pork Stock over the top of the roast, and add the sage and Italian parsley.

4. Roast the meat and onion uncovered at 325°F for 90 minutes or until the roast is cooked to an internal temperature of 145°F.

5. This dish pairs nicely with Maple Sage Roasted Butternut Squash (page 210).

Schweinshaxe, *a traditional German dish* that translates into "Pork Knuckles," is a rich and delicious broth made from the braised meat of the pig's front foreleg. Despite the unappealing name, people *love this dish.* And like many German dishes, the flavor is enhanced with a bit of booze; we just replace the glutenous beer with our favorite organic hard cider!

DIFFICULTY
Intermediate

TIME to TABLE
3-6 hours

SERVES
4-6

PREHEAT
Oven to 450°F

EQUIPMENT
Stockpot

INGREDIENTS

2 fresh ham hocks (also called pork knuckles)

2 carrots, cut into 2-inch pieces

3 celery stalks, cut into 2-inch pieces

1 medium yellow onion, quartered

1 leek, cut into 2-inch pieces

6 cloves garlic, crushed

1 teaspoon fennel seeds

1 teaspoon fresh rosemary, finely chopped

2 teaspoons salt

2 teaspoons peppercorns

4-6 cups Pork Stock (page 66)

3 tablespoons arrowroot powder

¼ cup organic hard cider (apple juice works, too)

½ teaspoon ground cumin

1 teaspoon fresh flat leaf Italian parsley, chopped

Zest of one lemon

SCHWEINSHAXE |STEWED HAM HOCKS|

1. In a large stockpot, combine the hocks with the carrots, celery, onion, leek, garlic, fennel seeds, rosemary, salt, and peppercorns.

2. Pour in enough Pork Stock to cover at least ⅔ of the pork.

3. Bring the liquid to a boil on the stovetop over high heat.

4. Reduce the heat to low, and cover. Simmer for 2 hours or until the meat is very tender.

5. Gently remove the hocks from the stock, and transfer them to a baking sheet. Roast them at 450°F for 30 minutes.

6. Meanwhile, strain the stock, and pour 3 cups into a small saucepan.

7. Cook the stock over medium heat until bubbling. Then, sift in the arrowroot powder, whisking constantly. This should slightly thicken the stock but will not turn it into gravy.

8. Transfer the hocks to a serving dish, and pour the sauce over the top.

9. Finish by pouring in the hard cider and sprinkling on the cumin, Italian parsley, and lemon zest.

This *famous Italian dish* is normally made with veal or lamb. Naturally, we wondered: why not pork? Must have been an oversight on the part of the Italians, because this version will not fail to please! Fit for Tuesday night dinner or the Queen, see how amazing it looks paired with our *Mashed Cauliflower* (page 208).

DIFFICULTY
Intermediate

TIME to TABLE
3-6 hours

SERVES
4-6

EQUIPMENT
Cheesecloth; kitchen twine; Dutch oven

INGREDIENTS

2 sprigs rosemary

2 sprigs thyme

3 whole cloves

2 bay leaves

½ cup blanched almond flour

2 tablespoons tapioca flour

1 teaspoon salt

¼ teaspoon black pepper

2 fresh ham shanks or hocks

2-3 tablespoons Lard (page 62)

1 cup yellow onions, diced

1 cup celery, diced

1 cup carrots, diced

⅔ cup white wine or apple juice

3 cups Pork Stock (page 66)

Juice of one lemon

2 tablespoons chopped fresh flat leaf Italian parsley

PORKO BUCCO

1. Create a cheesecloth bag with the rosemary, thyme, cloves, and bay leaves. Close with the twine, and set aside.

2. In a shallow bowl, combine the almond flour, tapioca flour, salt, and black pepper.

3. Coat all sides of the shanks with the flour mixture.

4. In a Dutch oven, melt the Lard, and brown each side of the pork over medium heat.

5. Remove the pork, set it aside, and add the onions, celery, and carrots to the hot pan, adding more Lard if needed.

6. Cook until the vegetables begin to soften, about 5 minutes.

7. Add the wine to deglaze the pan, gently scraping the bottom to remove any remaining bits of food.

8. Return the cooked shanks to the Dutch oven, and add the Pork Stock and cheesecloth bag. Bring to a boil.

9. Reduce the heat to low, and simmer covered for 4 hours or until the meat falls off of the bone.

10. Add the lemon juice and Italian parsley to finish and serve.

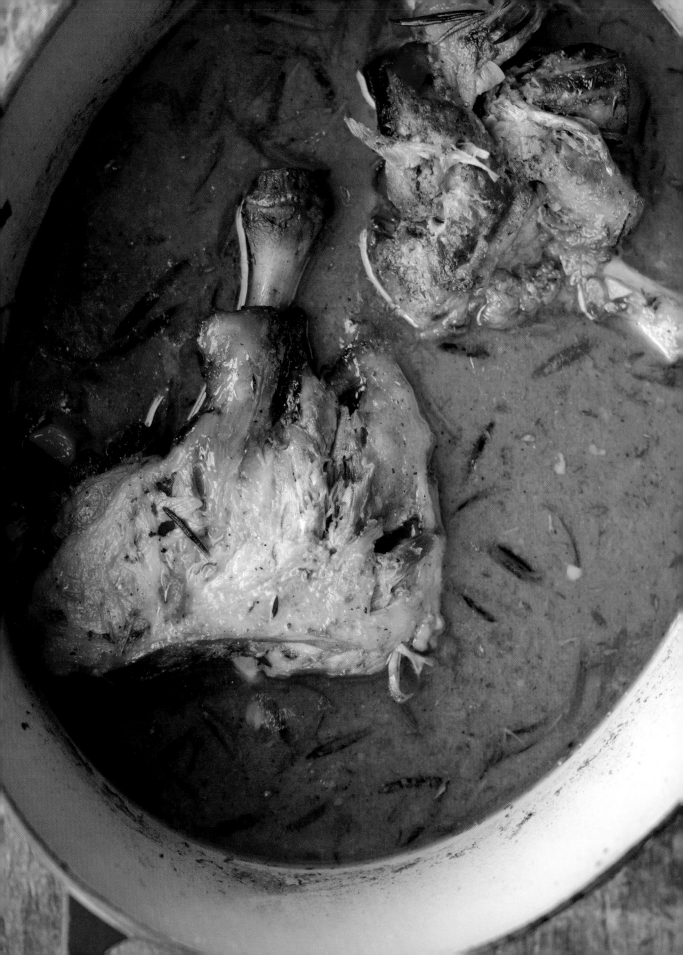

The best thing about pork belly is the contrast in textures between the *crispy skin* and the absolutely *juicy and tender* muscle meat. We honestly believe you'll question whether you really want to turn all that pork belly into bacon after you've made our Cracklin' Pork Belly or *Smoked Pork Belly* (page 96).

This incredibly rich dish is best served with some light green veggies. Just be sure to serve yourself first—there will be no leftovers!

DIFFICULTY
Easy

TIME TO TABLE
1-2 hours

SERVES
4-6

PREHEAT
Oven to 325°F

INGREDIENTS

2½ pounds pork belly

2 teaspoons salt

2 teaspoons chili powder

1 teaspoon ground coriander

1 teaspoon ground cumin

½ teaspoon cinnamon

⅛ teaspoon ground cloves

1 teaspoon black pepper

CRACKLIN' PORK BELLY

1. Pat the outside of the meat dry with a towel.

2. Make your rub by combining the salt, chili powder, coriander, cumin, cinnamon, cloves, and black pepper in a small bowl.

3. With a sharp knife, make shallow cuts into the skin of the pork in a crisscross pattern. If your butcher has sliced the belly for you, this isn't necessary.

4. Completely cover the outside of the prepared meat with the rub.

5. Place the meat on a baking sheet, skin side up, and roast it at 325°F for about 90 minutes or until the skin has become slightly browned and there is a tender give to the meat. The internal temperature should be about 145°F.

6. Let cool. Cut into bite-size pieces to serve.

Note: **You might see a nipple on the skin of your belly. Don't freak out; it's perfectly edible. But if it grosses you out, feel free to remove it with a paring knife.**

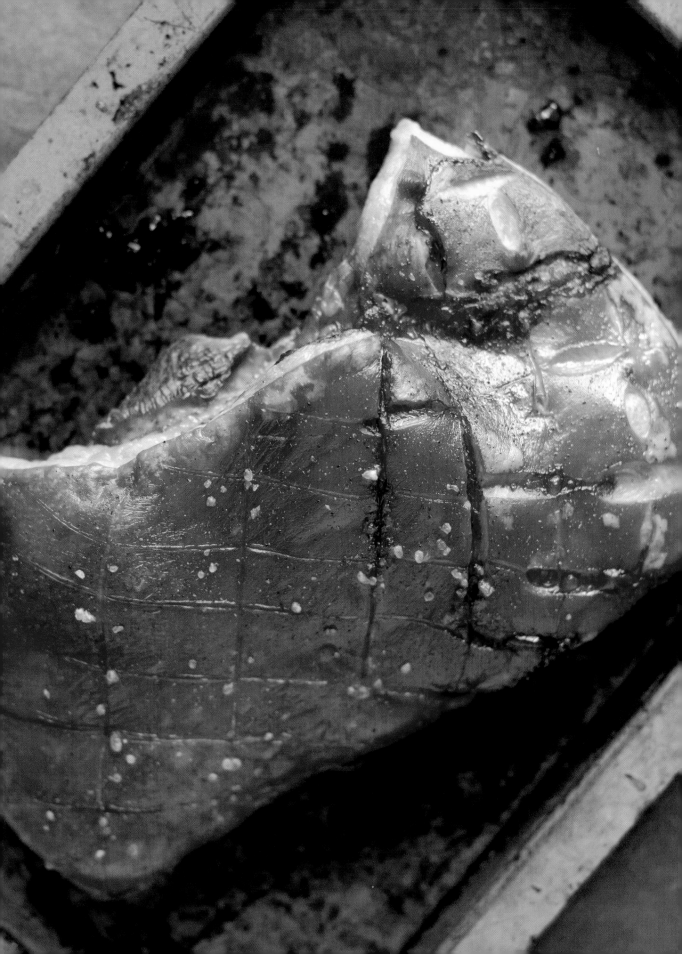

The sweetness of apples pairs beautifully with juicy pork tenderloin, and adding *some spicy ginger* doubles the effect. Even better: the apples become a complimentary sauce for your slices of tenderloin. Our children love this recipe, and it's simple enough that little hands can help you prepare it.

DIFFICULTY
Intermediate

TIME to TABLE
1-2 hours

SERVES
2-4

PREHEAT
Oven to 350°F

INGREDIENTS

4 apples, peeled and thinly sliced (honeycrisp recommended)

¼ cup unsweetened applesauce

1 teaspoon freshly grated or ground ginger (fresh preferred)

½ teaspoon salt

½ teaspoon ground allspice

⅛ teaspoon black pepper

1 pound pork tenderloin

APPLE GINGER TENDERLOIN

1. Spread the sliced apples over the bottom of a 13 x 9-inch baking dish, reserving about ½ cup for the top of the tenderloin. The thicker you slice the apples, the more juicy and similar to a baked apple texture they will be.

2. In a bowl, combine the applesauce with the ginger, salt, allspice, and black pepper. Set the mixture aside.

3. Place the tenderloin on top of the bed of apples, and spread the applesauce mixture on top.

4. Set the remaining apple slices on top of the meat.

5. Roast the tenderloin at 350°F for 40-50 minutes. Ideally, your tenderloin will still be slightly pink in the center with an internal temperature of about 145°F.

6. Serve the tenderloin with something acidic or slightly bitter to balance out the sweetness of the dish. We recommend a light salad with a good balsamic dressing like our Prosciutto & Fig Salad (page 236).

Note: **This recipe can easily be doubled and cooked together, since you will probably want leftovers!**

DIFFICULTY
Easy

TIME to TABLE
3-6 hours

SERVES
6-8

PREHEAT
Oven to 325°F

INGREDIENTS

1 tablespoon salt

1 tablespoon chili powder

1 teaspoon ground cumin

1 teaspoon smoked paprika

¼ teaspoon black pepper

5 pounds pork shoulder roast, Boston butt or picnic

½ cup Lard (page 62), melted

½ cup apple cider vinegar

Every week we prepare one of these shoulders. Sounds excessive, but there are few things you can prepare as easily with such *amazing results*. Our friends and family request this nearly every time we invite them over. When it's finished cooking, simply shred the meat and you'll have pounds and pounds of pork to snack on or use in other dishes, like our *Pork Tamales* (page 180) and *Porktastic Frittata* (page 152).

SLOW ROASTED SHOULDER

1. In a small bowl, combine the salt, chili powder, cumin, smoked paprika, and black pepper with a fork.

2. Dry off the shoulder with a towel and rub the outside of the pork shoulder with the spice mixture.

3. In a separate bowl, whisk together the Lard and apple cider vinegar.

4. Roast the pork, fat side up, in a baking dish at 325°F for about 4 hours. Baste with the re-whisked vinegar mixture every 30-45 minutes. After about 3 hours, check to make sure the meat is still tender to the touch; this will prevent it from drying out. As soon as the meat begins to firm up and pull apart easily, remove it from the heat. For ultimate juiciness and tenderness, the internal temperature should reach about 185°F.

5. When the meat has finished roasting, shred it with two forks. If your pork is too dry, reincorporate some of the liquid left in the baking sheet as you shred it.

DIFFICULTY
Basic

TIME TO TABLE
Less than 12 hours

SERVES
8-12

PREHEAT
Oven to 300°F

EQUIPMENT
Large Dutch oven

INGREDIENTS

1 cup Pork Stock (page 66)

½ cup honey

1 cup pineapple or apple juice

1 teaspoon ground cloves

2 teaspoons salt

½ teaspoon onion powder

¼ teaspoon black pepper

5 pounds ham roast

1 fresh pineapple, cut into 2-inch chunks

Can you cure a holiday ham yourself and serve it to your family? *Absolutely!* Do you have six months to prepare? Perhaps not. Rather than wait that long for your ham to cure, we recommend this simpler, quicker dish that will invoke the pineapple and cherry flavors of traditional *holiday hams*. It's definitely a lot better than the gluten-and processed-sugar-packed store-bought versions. We served this dish for Christmas brunch and it was a huge hit!

HAWAIIAN PORK ROAST

1. In a large mixing bowl, whisk together the Pork Stock, honey, juice, cloves, salt, onion powder, and black pepper. This is your brining mixture.

2. Marinate the meat overnight (at least 8 hours) in the brining mixture.

3. When you're ready to roast the ham, remove it from the brining mixture (keep the brine for basting), and place it in a large Dutch oven on top of the pineapple chunks.

4. Roast the ham at 300°F for 3 hours, basting every 30 minutes with remaining brine.

5. To serve, shred the meat off of the bone, and transfer it to a serving bowl with the pineapple chunks. Our Sweet Potato Casserole (page 214) is a great accompaniment to this dish.

If you're squeamish about offal, tongue is a good place to start. Handling it raw might turn you off at first, but once it's cooked it looks like any shredded muscle meat—so much so that we've served it to guests without them knowing they were eating tongue! It also has a *milder flavor than liver or kidneys,* and is incredibly affordable. This recipe is perfect with *hot pepper sauce* and *Pork Tamales* (page 180).

DIFFICULTY
Intermediate

TIME TO TABLE
Over 8 hours

SERVES
2-4

EQUIPMENT
Slow cooker

INGREDIENTS

2 pork tongues or 2 pounds fatty roast*

1 cup Pork Stock (page 66)

1 tablespoon chili powder

2 teaspoons ground cumin

1 teaspoon sweet Hungarian paprika

1 teaspoon dried oregano

1 teaspoon salt

¼ teaspoon black pepper

⅛ teaspoon cayenne pepper

LENGUA CARNITAS |PORK TONGUE|

1. Ask your butcher to prepare the pork tongues for you. It's much easier for them to carefully slice off the silvery-colored skin from the top of each tongue. It makes the process a lot more tolerable. If the tongue arrives with the skin still on, we recommend leaving it on through the cooking process and removing it once the meat is tender. Then, it will lift off easily as you shred the muscle meat, and it won't leave a lingering taste of any kind. (It's just the texture that most don't like.)

2. Place the tongues, Pork Stock, chili powder, cumin, Hungarian paprika, oregano, salt, black pepper, and cayenne pepper into the slow cooker, and cook on low for 8 hours.

3. Shred the tongues and pan fry over medium heat to caramelize the meat.

4. Incorporate the left over broth into the meat for a juicy, moist, and delicious addition to lettuce or cabbage tacos.

*Tip: **You can use any fatty cut of roasting meat in this recipe. But be brave and bold—offal is great for you and this is a good place to start!**

144

Something about the pickles, mustard, ham, and pork combo in a *Cuban sandwich* gives it universal appeal. When we heard of something called a Porchetta—a pork belly wrapped around a roast or loin—it seemed like something that could only enhance the Cuban. How could double the pork not be good?

A tied pork roast—especially a pork belly— always impresses! Make a truly memorable meal by serving this dish with our *Cuban Spiced Plantains* (page 238).

DIFFICULTY
Intermediate

TIME TO TABLE
2-4 hours

SERVES
4-6

PREHEAT
Oven to 500°F

EQUIPMENT
Kitchen twine

INGREDIENTS

¼ cup yellow mustard

¼ cup chopped dill pickles or dill pickle relish

2 teaspoons ground cumin

2 teaspoons ground coriander

1 teaspoon salt

¼ teaspoon black pepper

2½ pounds pork belly

1½ pounds boneless pork roast or tenderloin

CUBAN PORCHETTA

1. In a small bowl, combine the mustard and pickles.

2. In a separate bowl, combine the cumin, coriander, salt, and black pepper.

3. Lay out the pork belly, skin side down, and sprinkle it with the spice mixture. Then, spread a thin layer of the mustard and pickles on the top of the belly.

4. Unfold the roast or tenderloin, and lay it on top of the belly. Sprinkle the inside of the roast with the spices, and evenly spread on the remaining mustard and pickles.

5. Starting with one outer edge of the meat, carefully roll everything into a round, and tie it tightly with kitchen twine. Since the meat will shrink as it cooks, the tighter you can tie the twine, the better.

6. Rub the remaining spices on the outside of the meat roll, and place it in a roasting dish on a raised rack so that the meat does not sit in its juices.

7. Roast the roll at 500°F for 30 minutes.

8. Without opening the oven door, reduce the oven temperature to 300°F, and continue to roast the meat for 90 more minutes or until the center temperature reaches 145°F. Once it has reached that temperature, remove it. Let it rest for 10-20 minutes before cutting off the twine. Then, slice and serve.

There are no special techniques or equipment required for the recipes in this section. That doesn't mean these dishes aren't equally delicious, or the flavors any less complex, you just won't need a fryer or Dutch oven to make them. In other words, while the preparations might be conventional, the results will be anything but!

CONVENTIONAL PREPARATIONS

DIFFICULTY
Advanced

TIME TO TABLE
1-2 hours

SERVES
4-6

PREHEAT
Oven to 425°F

EQUIPMENT
Individual oven-safe serving dishes

INGREDIENTS

2 tablespoons Lard (page 62)

½ cup yellow onions, diced

½ cup carrots, diced

½ cup celery, diced

½ cup mushrooms, diced

½ cup frozen peas

1 teaspoon dried tarragon

1 teaspoon dried thyme

13.5 ounce can full-fat coconut milk

2 tablespoons arrowroot powder

1 pound pork meat, cooked and diced (or ground)

6 Homestyle Biscuits, unbaked (page 218)

Our boys have a favorite book we read to them, titled *Piggie Pie*, about a witch outsmarted by the pigs she's attempting to capture for "Piggie Pie." When we told them we were going to do a book of pig recipes, the first thing they asked for was *Gritch the Witch's Piggie Pie*. We're pretty sure our version, with its creamy consistency, is more delicious than hers. If you miss the pre-Paleo days of pot pies and dumplings, this reinvented classic should satisfy those cravings in *a grain-free way!*

It's also a great way to use up any leftover meat or veggies in your fridge. Feel free to improvise with your own favorite vegetables, like broccoli and cauliflower. There's no need to serve this dish with anything else; Piggy Pot Pie is *a meal in itself!*

PIGGIE POT PIE

1. In a large skillet, melt Lard over medium heat.

2. Add the onions, carrots, celery, mushrooms, and peas (dice the veggies to about the size of the peas), and cook until softened, about 8 minutes.

3. Add the tarragon, thyme, and coconut milk (in that order), stirring to combine for about 1 minute.

4. Sift the arrowroot powder over the wet mixture, constantly whisking until the ingredients are thoroughly incorporated and slightly thickened, about 3 minutes.

5. Add the cooked pork, and stir to coat the pork with the sauce.

6. Reduce the heat to medium-low, and simmer uncovered for 10 minutes.

7. Transfer ¾ cup of the mixture into each of the 6 individual ovenproof containers, topping each with an unbaked biscuit. The biscuits should be able to sit nicely inside the containers, but the liquid mixture should have enough room to bubble under the biscuits. If you are using small ramekins, make sure to reduce the size of the biscuits accordingly.

8. Bake the pot pies uncovered at 425°F for 12 minutes. Since all of the ingredients are cooked except the biscuit, the pot pies will be ready when the biscuits are golden brown on the top with the liquid bubbling underneath it.

9. Serve warm with a spoon and Lard Butter (page 246).

DIFFICULTY
Basic

TIME to TABLE
Less than 45 minutes

SERVES
6-8

PREHEAT
Oven to 400°F

INGREDIENTS
12 eggs

½ cup full-fat coconut milk

1 pound Italian Sausage (loose) (page 82)

1 cup broccoli, diced

1 medium red onion, diced

2 garlic cloves, minced

1 teaspoon fresh flat leaf Italian parsley, chopped

1 teaspoon fresh oregano, chopped

During the holidays, we like to host *family brunches* rather than dinners. It's much easier to travel during the mornings and afternoons — especially if you have a few whiny children in tow! On these occasions, we like to feed our large family a big frittata.

You can make this recipe over and over again, varying the ingredients each time. It's fantastic with *pulled pork, crispy bacon, and homemade sausage*. Just gather leftover meat and veggies from your fridge, mix in the eggs and coconut milk, stick it in the oven, and walk away for 20 minutes. *Voila!* A perfect make-ahead dish. The leftovers make for a great snack or a quick breakfast on a frantic morning.

PORKTASTIC FRITTATA

1. In a large mixing bowl, beat together the eggs and coconut milk.

2. In a skillet, brown the sausage over medium heat.

3. With a slotted spoon, transfer the sausage from the skillet to a towel-covered plate.

4. Drain the fat from the skillet, except for 2 tablespoons.

5. Sauté the broccoli, onion, and garlic until the onion pieces are translucent, about 6 minutes.

6. Return the sausage to the skillet, and add the Italian parsley and oregano. Stir to combine.

7. Whisk the eggs and coconut milk together again until bubbly and frothy.

8. Pour the freshly whisked mixture over the top of the sausage, and transfer the skillet to the oven. Bake for 20 minutes at 400°F until the top just starts to brown.

DIFFICULTY
Intermediate

TIME TABLE
Less than an hour

SERVES
6-8

PREHEAT
Oven to 400°F

INGREDIENTS

1 cup English cucumber, diced

1½ teaspoons salt, divided

1 uncooked Lard Pie Crust (page 272)

1 pound ground pork

1 garlic clove, minced

½ tablespoon ground cumin

1 teaspoon ground coriander

¼ teaspoon black pepper

1 white onion, diced

6 eggs, beaten

1 tablespoon fresh dill, chopped

2 tablespoons full-fat coconut milk

Eggs are fantastic at absorbing flavors to mimic the experience of eating uniquely flavored dishes. And, in this case, eggs take on the taste of gyros. Our egg pie satisfies as both the main dish at a large brunch or as a week's worth of breakfasts. The crust is not required, but adds a nice touch for *a special Sunday morning*. And if you can tolerate dairy, feta cheese would be a fantastic addition.

CUCUMBER DILL QUICHE

1. In a small bowl, combine the cucumbers with 1 teaspoon of the salt, set the bowl aside for at least 10 minutes. This will allow the cucumbers to give up some of their moisture; you don't want a watery quiche!

2. Meanwhile, place the pie crust in a 9-inch pie plate. Prebake the crust at 400°F for 5 minutes or until the crust just begins to turn a golden brown.

3. In a large bowl, fully mix the ground pork with the garlic, cumin, coriander, black pepper, and remaining ½ teaspoon of the salt.

4. In a large skillet, brown the meat over medium heat. The spices should become aromatic, and the meat should be cooked through. Using a slotted spoon to ensure that the excess fat remains in the skillet, transfer the cooked meat to a mixing bowl.

5. In the same skillet, sauté the onion in the remaining fat over medium heat until it is softened and translucent, about 6 minutes. Add the diced onion to the meat mixture.

6. Strain the cucumber mixture, pressing gently to remove excess moisture and salt. Transfer the cucumbers to the mixing bowl, and toss together.

7. In a separate bowl, whisk the eggs, dill, and coconut milk together until bubbly and frothy. Add the mixture to the meat, and stir until all ingredients are evenly distributed.

8. Pour the mixture into the prebaked crust. If you have a crust protector, we recommend you use it to prevent the edges of the quiche from burning. You can also cut a circle out of aluminum foil to cover just the edge of the crust. Simply lay the foil over the top, but don't press down or the crust will crumble.

9. Smooth the top of the quiche with a spatula before putting it into the oven. Bake at 400°F for 40 minutes. The quiche will be done when a toothpick inserted into the center comes out clean. If it's a special occasion, top the quiche with a few slices of cucumber and a sprig of dill.

DIFFICULTY
Intermediate

TIME to TABLE
30-60 minutes

SERVES
4-6

PREHEAT
Oven to 350°F, boiling water to steam

INGREDIENTS

2½ pounds fresh, uncured ham steak (a 1-inch slice off a leg, bone and skin removed)

2 teaspoons salt

1 teaspoon black pepper

1 yellow onion, diced

2 garlic cloves, minced

⅓ cup olive oil

¼ cup white wine or apple juice

½ teaspoon cayenne pepper (optional)

2 pounds broccoli, chopped into bite-sized florets

1 spaghetti squash, halved, seeds removed

2 tablespoons Lard (page 62)

2 tablespoons fresh flat leaf Italian parsley, chopped

Tip: If you purchase ham that is already cured, skip to step 5.

This is a variation on a dish invented by Matt's grandfather. *The legend goes that* during a blizzard, when no one could leave the house, he made a meal out of what he could find in the kitchen: leftover ham, broccoli, and a box of pasta. The dish was a huge hit and entered the clan repertoire. Matt grew up eating this meal once a week and was eager to recreate it in a Paleo way, without the boxed pasta. As it turns out, substituting *spaghetti squash* actually makes the buttery lard and salty ham taste even better!

HAM AND BROCCOLI PASTA

1. Sprinkle both sides of the ham steak with the salt and black pepper.

2. Preheat a large skillet over medium-high heat.

3. Brown the ham on both sides, about 3 minutes per side.

4. Transfer the ham to a 350°F oven, and roast it for 30 minutes.

5. Allow the ham to cool. Then, dice it into ¼-inch cubes.

6. In a medium saucepan, sauté the onion and garlic in the olive oil over medium heat for 6 minutes or until the onion becomes translucent.

7. Add the wine and cayenne pepper, and cook for 1 minute.

8. Add the cooked ham to the saucepan, and stir. Simmer for 10 minutes.

9. With the cut side down, place the spaghetti squash halves in a shallow dish with ¼ inch of water.

10. Microwave the squash for 12 minutes or until a fork easily pushes all the way through. You can also place the cut side down on a baking sheet, and bake the squash in the oven at 350°F for 40 minutes.

11. Once cooked and softened, using a fork, scrape the inside of the squash to create the noodles, and place them in a serving bowl. Toss with the Lard.

12. Meanwhile, steam the broccoli florets over boiling water in a steaming basket for 8 minutes.

13. Pour the ham mixture and the broccoli on top of the spaghetti squash, and toss. Finish with the parsley, and add salt and pepper to taste.

DIFFICULTY
Basic

TIME to TABLE
Under 30 minutes

SERVES
2-4

INGREDIENTS

2 tablespoons Lard (page 62)

½ cup yellow onions, diced

½ cup carrots, medium diced

½ cup celery, medium diced

½ cup mushrooms, diced

½ cup broccoli, medium diced

3 cloves garlic, minced

1 cup cubed or ground pork, precooked

1 tablespoon coconut aminos

2 teaspoons fish sauce (Red Boat brand preferred)

Fresh herbs (optional)

For those on an autoimmune protocol of the Paleo diet, breakfast can be the hardest meal of the day. Eliminating cereal and bread is hard enough, but when you can't eat nuts and eggs breakfast starts to feel impossible. We created this recipe to solve just that problem. It's free of any problematic ingredients and still manages to be fulfilling. Stacy loves to add this to a cup of *Pork Stock* (page 66) almost every morning. It's an incredibly *nutrient-dense way* to start your day, and a great way to use up leftover vegetables!

VEGGIE STIR-FRY WITH CUBED PORK

1. In a large skillet, melt the Lard over medium heat. Then, add the onions, carrots, celery, mushrooms, broccoli, and garlic, and sauté until the veggies are softened, about 6 minutes.

2. Add the pork, coconut aminos, fish sauce, and herbs, and stir to distribute the ingredients evenly.

3. Toss the ingredients in the pan as you continue to cook for 5 minutes to incorporate the flavors before serving.

DIFFICULTY
Intermediate

TIME to TABLE
Under 30 minutes

SERVES
4

PREHEAT
Oven to 350°F

INGREDIENTS

4 rib chops, bones removed, about ¾ inch thick

½ cup olive oil

1 cup blanched almond flour

2 teaspoons salt

1 teaspoon smoked paprika

½ teaspoon dried or fresh tarragon, chopped

½ teaspoon onion powder

½ teaspoon garlic powder

¼ teaspoon white pepper

Tip: The cooking time will vary depending on the thickness of the chops, so be sure to check them frequently as they cook.

In 1965, Shake 'n Bake hit the market, offering busy moms (dads didn't cook so much back then) a faster and "healthier" option to fried chicken. It was so easy, the marketing went, that kids could help to cook it: just stick meat in a bag of ingredients, shake it up, and stick it in the oven. Unfortunately, those boxes of ingredients were full of chemicals, not to mention the grain-based coating.

Well, guess what? Baking pork chops is so easy you don't need a shortcut! And our grain-free version recaptures all that *childhood shake and bake magic* without the bad ingredients. We like to top them with our *Liver Gravy* (page 252), which turns the dish into something similar to a classic Schnitzel.

SHAKEN & BAKED PORK CHOPS

1. Pat the chops dry with a towel to enhance adhesion.

2. Pour the olive oil into a flat-bottomed bowl.

3. Combine the almond flour, salt, smoked paprika, tarragon, onion powder, garlic powder, and white pepper in a large plastic bag or bowl. Be sure to mix the ingredients well so that the spices are evenly distributed.

4. Dip each chop into the oil, and shake off the excess so that only a thin coating is left. Place each chop in the plastic bag or bowl one at a time, and coat with the breading. If the chops are too oily, remove any wet chunks from the flour mixture.

5. Place the chops onto a baking sheet, preferably raised on a rack to allow the chops to cook evenly on all sides, and bake at 350°F for about 20 minutes, or until the internal cooking temperature is between 140 and 160°F (depending on your preference for slightly pink or well done).

This *summer dish* is one of the best ways to show off home-cured pancetta: *the creamy spaghetti squash* and *bright asparagus* perfectly highlight the meat's complex and salty flavor. This dish manifested itself to us during a visit to our Farmers' Market, but feel free to adapt it to any seasonal produce, like winter root vegetables.

DIFFICULTY
Intermediate

TIME to TABLE
30-60 minutes

SERVES
4-6

INGREDIENTS

4 tablespoons Lard (page 62), divided

1 pound asparagus, ends removed and cut into ½-inch pieces

1 yellow onion, diced

2 garlic cloves, minced

1 pound homemade Pancetta (page 70), diced

¼ cup white wine or apple juice

1 teaspoon sweet Hungarian paprika

½ teaspoon dry mustard

½ teaspoon salt

¼ teaspoon white pepper

¼ teaspoon red pepper flakes (optional)

1 medium spaghetti squash, cut in half, seeds removed

1 tablespoon fresh flat leaf Italian parsley, chopped

Tip: If you snap one of your asparagus in half by hand, it will show you the natural place to remove the end of that bunch. Then simply cut off the remaining pieces in the bundle at about the same place!

PANCETTA AND ASPARAGUS PASTA

1. In a medium saucepan, melt 2 tablespoons of the Lard over medium heat.

2. Sauté the asparagus, onion, and garlic, stirring occasionally, until the onion turns translucent, about 6 minutes.

3. Add the pancetta, and continue to cook for another 3 minutes.

4. Add the wine, Hungarian paprika, dry mustard, salt, white pepper, and red pepper flakes to the pan, and allow the mixture to bubble for 2 minutes.

5. Reduce the heat to low, cover the pan, and simmer for 15 minutes.

6. Meanwhile, place the spaghetti squash in a shallow dish with ¼ inch of water. Place the dish in the microwave, and cook on high for 10-15 minutes or until the squash is easily pierced by a fork. You can also use a conventional oven: place the squash, cut side down, on a baking sheet, and bake at 350°F for 40 minutes.

7. Gently scoop out the inside of the squash with a fork, forming your noodles, and place the noodles in a serving dish. Toss with the remaining 2 tablespoons of Lard.

8. Pour the pancetta sauce over the top of the squash, and toss with Italian parsley before serving.

DIFFICULTY
Basic

TIME to TABLE
30-60 minutes

SERVES
4

INGREDIENTS

2 tablespoons Lard (page 62)

4 rib chops, ½-inch thick

1 teaspoon salt

⅛ teaspoon pepper

1 yellow onion, sliced

2 cups tomatoes, diced (or 1 15.5 ounce can)

½ teaspoon dried thyme

½ teaspoon dried oregano

½ teaspoon dried marjoram

½ teaspoon dried basil

¼ teaspoon red pepper flakes (optional)

1 tablespoon fresh flat leaf Italian parsley, chopped

Matt created this dish long before he went Paleo and became a stay-at-home dad moonlighting as a recipe developer. In those early days, he fumbled his way around the kitchen, grabbing canned goods and boxed pasta, hoping something edible would result. Over the years, we've taken the lovely, *traditional Italian* flavors he ultimately mastered and paired them with Paleo-friendly meats. Instead of pasta, we suggest subtly sweet *Sautéed Cabbage* (page 228) or *Turnip & Parsnip Purée* (page 224).

ITALIAN TOMATO PORK CHOP

1. In a large skillet, melt the Lard over medium heat.

2. Meanwhile, season the pork chops with salt and pepper, and sear them until they are light brown on each side, about 2 minutes per side.

3. Remove the chops from the skillet, and set aside.

4. Add the onion to the same pan, and cook it until it just begins to soften, about 5 minutes.

5. Add the tomatoes, thyme, oregano, marjoram, basil, and red pepper flakes, and stir.

6. Cover, and reduce the heat to medium-low. Simmer to combine the flavors and soften the tomatoes, about 15 minutes.

7. Return the chops to the skillet, and cover the skillet to finish cooking, about 5 minutes, or until the internal temperature reaches about 140°F.

8. Keep it rustic by serving the chops in the skillet. Or, for a more formal occasion, let the chops sit for 5 minutes before slicing and plating them with the sauce. Top the chops with the Italian parsley.

DIFFICULTY
Intermediate

TIME & TABLE
30-60 minutes

SERVES
4

PREHEAT

4 bone-in pork chops, 1 inch thick

2 tablespoons Lard (page 62)

1 bunch kale, stem removed (about 1 pound)

⅓ cup chopped pistachios, toasted

1 garlic clove, minced

½ teaspoon ground coriander

Juice and zest of ½ lemon

Salt and pepper to taste

Kale is a *wonderful food* that too many people avoid thanks to its bad reputation for tasting bitter. Fortunately, the real food movement has given new life to this nutrient-dense vegetable. Kale has more bioavailable calcium than milk, more Vitamin A than broccoli, and more Vitamin C than an apple! And cooking it into something delicious is a lot easier than you probably think. We like to stuff lard-sautéed kale into a pork chop for an elegant surprise. It's absolutely delicious, *and packs a nutritional wallop!*

KALE & PISTACHIO STUFFED PORK CHOPS

1. Ask your butcher to "pocket" the chops for you (it shouldn't cost you extra). If you need to do it yourself, however, use a 4-6-inch knife to pierce the fatty side of the chop. Then, gently wiggle the knife side to side until the "pocket" is about 5 inches long and 3 inches wide.

2. In a medium pan (we recommend a cast-iron skillet or Dutch oven), melt the Lard over medium-high heat.

3. Cook the kale until it is slightly wilted, about 5 minutes.

4. Add the toasted pistachios, garlic, coriander, lemon juice, and lemon zest to the kale, tossing to fully distribute the ingredients, about 2 minutes.

5. Remove the kale mixture from the heat, transfer it to a bowl, and set aside.

6. Add salt and pepper to taste to each side of the pork chops. Stuff the chops with as much of the cooked kale as you are able, and use a skewer or toothpick to seal the kale inside the chops. (You should have about half the stuffing left over).

7. Sear the pork chops over medium-high in the hot pan, about 4-5 minutes per side.

8. Transfer the skillet to a 350°F oven, and bake the chops uncovered for 30 minutes or until the centers of the chops reach 140°F.

9. Remove the chops from the heat, and let them rest for 5 minutes.

10. Warm the remaining stuffing, and spoon it on top of each chop before serving.

Everyone needs a *"company" dish*—the one that impresses the guests. This meal manages to provide that *Wow Factor* without demanding hours of cooking. Stick it on fine china and it will look like you spent the whole day in the kitchen.

DIFFICULTY
Intermediate

TIME TO TABLE
30-60 minutes

SERVES
4

PREHEAT
Oven to 350°F

INGREDIENTS

4 bone-in pork chops, 1 inch thick

2 tablespoons Lard (page 62)

2 medium baking apples (Gala and York are our favorites), peeled, cored, and diced into ½-inch cubes

10 strips bacon, diced

1 red onion, diced

2 garlic cloves, minced

4 fresh sage leaves, finely chopped

¼ teaspoon sweet Hungarian paprika

1 tablespoon lemon juice

Salt and pepper to taste

Tip: Dicing the ingredients the same size helps them to cook evenly.

APPLE & BACON STUFFED PORK CHOPS

1. Ask your butcher to pocket the pork chops for you. If you have to do it yourself, use a 4-6-inch knife to pierce the fatty side of the chops. Then, gently wiggle the knife side to side until the "pocket" is about 5 inches long and 3 inches wide.

2. In a medium pan (we recommend a cast-iron skillet or Dutch oven), melt the Lard over medium-high heat.

3. Cook the apples, bacon, and onion until the onion is softened and the bacon is crispy, about 8 minutes.

4. Add the garlic, sage, Hungarian paprika, and lemon juice to the pan, and toss as the stuffing cooks, about 2 minutes.

5. Remove the apple stuffing from the heat, transfer it to a bowl, and set it aside.

6. Add salt and pepper to each side of the pork chops, stuff them with as much apple stuffing as you can, and use a skewer or toothpick to seal the stuffing inside. (You should have about half the stuffing left over.)

7. Sear the pork chops in the hot pan over medium-high heat, about 4-5 minutes per side.

8. Transfer the skillet to a 350°F oven, and bake the pork chops uncovered for 30 minutes or until the centers of the chops reach 140°F.

9. Remove the chops from the heat, and let them rest for 5 minutes. Warm the remaining stuffing, and spoon it on top of each chop before serving.

A medium rare steak used to be our go-to dish for *all special occasions*. Trouble is, once we switched to grass-fed and pastured animals, the flavor of the beef changed and a steak just didn't have the same appeal, especially with the associated price tag. But since we figured out how to make the *perfect pork chop*, we don't even think about steak anymore. You will be amazed at how simple it is to cook a pork chop, making it great for entertaining or as an end-of-day pick-me-up! And, unlike beef, pastured pork has a flavor that enhances the *"pigness of the pig,"* as Joel Salatin would say, rather than changing to a gamey flavor.

DIFFICULTY
Basic

TIME TO TABLE
Under 30 minutes

SERVES
4

PREHEAT
Oven to 350°F

EQUIPMENT
Cast iron skillet

INGREDIENTS
½ teaspoon salt

½ teaspoon sweet Hungarian paprika

½ teaspoon garlic powder

¼ teaspoon black pepper

4 pork loins or rib chops, ½ inch to ¾-inch thick

PERFECT PORK CHOPS

1. In a small bowl, combine the salt, Hungarian paprika, garlic powder, and black pepper with a fork.

2. Sprinkle both sides of the chops with the spice mixture.

3. In a large skillet over medium-high heat, sear each side of the chops until the meat is slightly browned and the fat begins to caramelize, about 3-4 minutes per side, depending on thickness.

4. Transfer the pan to the oven preheated to 350°F, and roast the chops an additional 10 minutes or until the centers of the chops reach about 145°F (or more depending on how well done you prefer).

5. Remove the chops from the heat, and allow them to finish cooking in the pan, about 10 minutes.

DIFFICULTY
Basic

TIME *to* **TABLE**
1-2 hours

SERVES
4-6

PREHEAT
Oven to 350°F

INGREDIENTS

2 tablespoons Lard (page 62)

½ cup yellow onions, diced into ½-inch pieces

½ cup mushrooms, diced into ½-inch pieces

½ cup celery, diced into ½-inch pieces

½ cup carrots, diced into ½-inch pieces

2 pounds ground pork

½ pound ground pork liver or pork kidney (optional)

2 eggs

½ cup blanched almond flour

2 teaspoons fresh oregano, chopped

2 teaspoons fresh flat leaf Italian parsley, chopped

1 teaspoon sweet Hungarian paprika

1 teaspoon salt

½ teaspoon black pepper

½ cup tomato sauce (for the top)

When you find yourself at a loss on a weekday night, instead of picking up the phone and ordering takeout, why not make a *juicy meatloaf packed with vegetables?* With ground pork in plentiful supply (we tend to get up to 30 pounds off of one pig!), this is a relatively *low-prep meal*—so much so, we serve it once a week. It's also, yes, "insanely awesome," and that's according to our children and recipe testers. This is not the dried out, tasteless meatloaf of your youth—*give it a shot!*

INSANELY AWESOME MEATLOAF

1. In a large skillet, melt the Lard over medium-high heat.

2. Sauté the onions, mushrooms, celery, and carrots for about 8 minutes, stirring occasionally, until the onions are translucent. (Dicing the veggies small and keeping them a uniform size will help them cook quickly and evenly.) Remove the skillet from the heat.

3. In a large mixing bowl, combine the ground meats, eggs, almond flour, oregano, Italian parsley, Hungarian paprika, salt, black pepper, and cooked vegetables with your hands (your best kitchen utensil).

4. Press the mixture into a 4 x 9-inch loaf pan. Smooth the top, and spread the tomato sauce over it with a spatula. If you do not want or like tomatoes, try topping with a few strips of bacon instead!

5. Bake the meatloaf at 350°F for 60-70 minutes or until it is cooked through.

Tip: Double this recipe to ensure leftovers, or freeze one of them for an emergency dinner. You can also use this recipe to make meatballs, or cook them in silicon baking cups for lunches and snacks! Meatloaf is also a great way to incorporate organ meats into your diet. There's much going on here, subduing the unfamiliar taste of liver or even kidney!

In Stacy's family, Stuffed Bell Peppers are a *classic dish*. Rina, her *Italian* grandmother, made them for her *Hungarian* husband, Art; it was the perfect marriage of their two cultures. Rina passed before she could test this recipe, but we think she'd give it a big thumbs-up. The cauliflower rice is surprisingly perfect with the ground meat, and who doesn't love a topping of *caramelized tomato sauce?*

DIFFICULTY
Intermediate

TIME to TABLE
1-2 hours

SERVES
4-6

PREHEAT
Oven to 350°F

EQUIPMENT
Food processor or blender, muffin tin

INGREDIENTS

1½ cups cauliflower florets, stems removed

2 tablespoons Lard (page 62)

1 yellow onion, diced

2 cloves garlic, minced

1 pounds ground pork

1 pounds ground red meat (beef, venison, or bison)

2 cups diced tomatoes, fresh or canned (juice strained)

2 teaspoons salt

½ teaspoon fresh thyme, chopped

½ teaspoon ground coriander

½ teaspoon dried oregano

1 teaspoon sweet Hungarian paprika

¼ teaspoon black pepper

6 bell peppers, tops, seeds and ribs removed

½ cup tomato sauce

STUFFED BELL PEPPERS

1. In a food processor or blender, pulse the cauliflower florets into rice-sized pieces, usually about 10 pulses for 2 seconds in a food processor. Transfer the cauliflower to a large mixing bowl.

2. Melt the Lard in a medium skillet over medium heat.

3. Add the onion and garlic to the skillet, and sauté for about 5 minutes until the onions are translucent but not burned. Add the onion and garlic to the mixing bowl with the cauliflower.

4. Brown the ground meat in the same skillet over medium heat.

5. When completely browned, remove the skillet from the heat, strain most of the liquid, and transfer the meat to the mixing bowl.

6. In the mixing bowl, stir in the diced tomatoes, salt, thyme, coriander, oregano, Hungarian paprika, and black pepper. Continue to mix until all ingredients are thoroughly incorporated. Allow the mixture to sit for 5-10 minutes. The cauliflower should soak up the juices from the tomatoes and meat, but strain any remaining excess liquid.

7. Spoon the meat mixture into the uncooked bell peppers. Press the mixture down, packing into each pepper, and drain any liquid that surfaces. Fill the remaining space within each pepper, and press again until the peppers are fully packed.

8. Top each of the peppers with 1 tablespoon of tomato sauce, covering every part of the meat mixture.

9. Set the peppers in the cups of a muffin tin (it helps them to stand upright as they cook), and bake them at 350°F for 1 hour.

10. Serve with any remaining meat mixture and warmed tomato sauce, if desired. In our house, we fight over the extra meat!

DIFFICULTY
Intermediate

TIME TO TABLE
1-2 hours

SERVES
4-6

PREHEAT
Oven to 400°F

INGREDIENTS

½ head medium sized cabbage (about 4 cups)

1 lemon

6 garlic cloves

1 yellow onion

1 whole chicken, about 4 pounds, innards removed

1 tablespoon salt

½ teaspoon black pepper

1 sprig rosemary

10 strips of thick cut quality Bacon (page 68), cut in half

Note: Save your chicken innards for a delicious gravy, or add them to your next batch of broth to give yourself a super food boost!

Yes, the title of the book is *Beyond Bacon*, but, like every other sane person, we can't resist bacon either. And it's not just great on its own; it enhances just about any other food it's paired with—whether it's chicken or the cabbage in this recipe, which soaks up all the *wonderful juices* in the pan. Don't just take our word for it: *Bacon Chicken* is an *award-winning* recipe that has been featured in national publications. Most importantly, this elegant dish is relatively easy to make, yet always impresses.

BACON CHICKEN

1. Slice the cabbage into ¼-inch ribbons.

2. Halve the lemon and garlic cloves, quarter the onion (does not need to be peeled). Set them aside.

3. Pat the outside of the chicken dry with a towel.

4. Sprinkle salt and black pepper inside the chicken cavity, and rub the seasoning gently into the skin.

5. Stuff the chicken cavity with the lemon, onion, garlic and rosemary. If you are concerned about keeping the cavity closed, use twine to tie together the legs and tail.

6. Place the bacon slices over the entire exposed surface of the chicken, wrapping evenly in a single layer, ensuring that none of the chicken skin is left exposed. If the bacon doesn't stick, pat the chicken dry again, and start over. If you're able, weave the bacon in a lattice formation on the chicken, which will help prevent any pieces from falling off as the chicken cooks.

7. Spread the sliced cabbage evenly across the bottom of an ovenproof pan or baking dish (cast-iron works great). No fat or seasoning is required; the chicken will do all the work.

8. Set the prepared chicken on top of the cabbage, and roast it uncovered at 400°F for 90 minutes or until the chicken is cooked through. Stir the cabbage halfway through cooking to prevent it from burning. Some cabbage will brown slightly, but this will add flavor.

9. Let the dish rest for 10 minutes before serving.

A lot of people call this "*breakfast pasta*," but you can have it any time. It's one of the meals we serve when we're trying to convince people that eating Paleo doesn't require as much sacrifice as they might think. And really, what are you sacrificing when you can eat cream sauce *and* bacon without guilt?

DIFFICULTY
Intermediate

TIME to TABLE
30-60 minutes

SERVES
4-6

PREHEAT
Oven to 350°F

INGREDIENTS

1 medium spaghetti squash

¾ pound bacon

1 tablespoon arrowroot powder

½ cup full-fat coconut milk

6 eggs

1 teaspoon dried basil

1 teaspoon dried oregano

1 teaspoon dried marjoram

1 teaspoon dried parsley

1 teaspoon salt

¼ teaspoon garlic powder

1 tablespoon Lard (page 62)

1 tablespoon fresh flat leaf Italian parsley, chopped

SPAGHETTI ALLA CARBONARA

1. Cut the spaghetti squash in half, scoop out the seeds, and place the pieces open side down on a plate. Microwave the squash for 10 minutes. Alternatively, place the cut side down on a baking sheet, and bake the squash at 350°F for 40 minutes.

2. While the squash is cooking, fry the strips of bacon (whole) in a large skillet over medium heat. Use a cast-iron skillet or other skillet that you could also use for scrambling eggs.

3. When the bacon is finished cooking and crispy, remove it from the pan, and set it aside on a plate or rack covered with a towel. This will allow the fat to be absorbed and crisp the bacon further.

4. Over medium heat, whisk the arrowroot powder into the bacon grease, and cook for 2 minutes.

5. While the arrowroot cooks, combine the coconut milk, eggs, basil, oregano, marjoram, parsley, salt, and garlic powder in a bowl using a whisk. Continue mixing until all yolks are fully incorporated.

6. Pour the eggs into the bacon pan, and cook, stirring frequently, in the bacon fat until the eggs are still wet but cooked through, about 4 minutes. Transfer the mixture to a mixing bowl to stop cooking. (Do not overcook the eggs, or it will no longer be a creamy sauce.)

7. Slice the bacon into ½-inch strips, and add the bacon to the egg mixture.

8. Scoop out the spaghetti squash "noodles" with a fork, and add them to a serving bowl, tossing them with the Lard until it is fully melted.

9. Add the egg and bacon mixture to the noodle serving bowl.

10. Add Italian parsley to the bowl, and toss to combine all ingredients before serving.

DIFFICULTY
Intermediate

TIME to TABLE
30-60 minutes

SERVES
4-6

EQUIPMENT
Steamer

INGREDIENTS

HOT PEPPER SAUCE

1-3 dried chili de arbol (red chilies)

5 dried chipotle peppers

2 Pork Stock (page 66)

TAMALES

2 cups cauliflower florets, yellow preferred

2 tablespoons Lard (page 62)

½ cup red onion, diced

2 garlic cloves, minced

2 pounds shredded cooked pork from our Slow-Roasted Shoulder (page 140), Smoked Pulled Pork Shoulder (page 92) or Pork Lengua Carnitas (page 144)

2 large banana leaves, cut to 10 x 10-inch squares

Tamales are a *specialty Mexican food* with a big emphasis on corn: the meat is wrapped in corn meal dough, then steamed in cornhusks. For people with delicate digestion, all that corn can wreak havoc. Rather than risk it, we found alternatives — cauliflower and banana leaves — that result in the same *spicy deliciousness!*

PORK TAMALES

1. To make the Hot Pepper Sauce, slice open the peppers, and remove all stems and seeds. If you prefer your tamales less spicy, use fewer peppers. (Three peppers should be enough to pucker the face of braver spice lovers!) Then, wash your hands before you touch anything, especially your face!

2. Place the peppers and water in a bowl, and microwave for 7 minutes. Alternatively, simmer them in a small saucepan over medium heat for 15 minutes.

3. Blend the warmed peppers and Pork Stock together in a blender or food processor until smooth. Be aware that these peppers are serious business and will put off capsaicin fumes into the air as you cook and blend them. If someone in your house is sensitive or has an autoimmune condition, do this when they aren't around, as capsaicin is an immune system agitator.

4. In a food processor, pulse the cauliflower until the pieces are rice-sized, about 10 pulses for 2 seconds.

5. To assemble the tamales, begin by melting the Lard in a skillet over medium heat.

6. Add the onion and garlic to the skillet, and sauté them until soft, about 6 minutes. Remove from the heat.

7. In a large mixing bowl, combine the cooked pork, riced cauliflower, cooked onion, and one cup of the Hot Pepper Sauce.

8. Spread ¾ to 1 cup of the mixture in the center of an approximately 10 x 10-inch piece of banana leaf. Fold the top and bottom edges of the leaf into the center followed by the two sides. Seal the tamale as a tight package with a length of butcher twine.

9. Repeat step 8 until the rest of the mixture is used. Makes 6-8 tamales.

10. Place the tamales in a steamer or steaming basket over boiling water, and steam them for 20 minutes.

11. Serve them warm out of the steamer with the remaining Hot Pepper Sauce, meat, and guacamole.

Note: We found all the specialty ingredients for this recipe at our local Asian food market for very little money. The banana leaves are usually found in the frozen section. You'll pay only a few dollars for a large batch that will make many, many tamales!

DIFFICULTY
Basic

TIME TO TABLE
30-60 minutes

SERVES
6-8

PREHEAT
Oven to 325°F

INGREDIENTS

2 tablespoons Lard (page 62), divided

½ cup white onion, diced

1 pound ground pork

1 pound ground beef

1 pound ground lamb

½ cup blanched almond flour

4 egg yolks

1 teaspoon salt

½ teaspoon black pepper

½ teaspoon ground allspice

½ teaspoon ground nutmeg

Tip: Double the recipe for leftovers. Meatballs make excellent, on-the-go snacks!

In Sweden these meatballs are traditionally served with lingonberry jam and contain fillers like wheat binders. This version provides the flavors you miss without the hard to find ingredients or junk. You can top them with our creamy *Liver Gravy* (page 252), which gives you all of the super-nutrients of liver, without the off-putting taste and texture. Pair them with *Mashed Cauliflower* (page 208) and cranberry relish for a close to authentic experience. You can also stick them in a crockpot with tomato sauce and you have the perfect party food!

SWEDISH MEATBALLS

1. In a large pan, melt 1 tablespoon of the Lard over medium heat.

2. Add the onion, and cook it until transparent, about 6 minutes.

3. Remove the pan from the heat, and allow the onion to cool slightly.

4. Combine the onion, meats, blanched almond flour, egg yolks, salt, black pepper, allspice, and nutmeg using your hands.

5. Roll the meat mixture into 1-inch balls, approximately 1 heaping tablespoon each.

6. Using the same pan as the one used for the onion, melt the remaining 1 tablespoon of the Lard, and sear the meatballs over medium-high heat, cooking in batches and adding more Lard if needed to prevent the pan from drying out. Cook the meatballs until they are browned on all sides but not cooked through the center, about 3-4 minutes on each side. If you intend to make our Liver Gravy (page 252), reserve the pan drippings to add flavor to the gravy.

7. Place the meatballs in a baking dish, and finish cooking them in the preheated oven, about 10 minutes.

Frying food is one of the most intense experiences you can have in the kitchen. A lot of people avoid it because of the physical dangers (very hot fat!), or because it's so easy to burn your food if you don't know what you're doing. But once you get the hang of it, you'll never look back.

We recommend rendering back fat into lard (as described on page 62) for all your frying needs. Lard is stable at high temperatures and has a relatively high smoke point (over 375°F) compared to what you'd find in the vegetable oils that restaurants use. Not to mention, lard from pigs has that unbeatable porky taste!

FRIED LARD GOODNESS

DIFFICULTY
Advanced

TIME to TABLE
Under 30 minutes

SERVES
4-6

PREHEAT
Frying oil to 350°F

EQUIPMENT
Electric Fryer or heavy-bottomed pot

INGREDIENTS

¾ cup tapioca flour, divided

½ cup blanched almond flour

1 tablespoon arrowroot powder

1 teaspoon turmeric

½ teaspoon salt

2 egg yolks

¼ cup water

6 hot dogs, uncured recommended

Lard (page 62) for frying

Note: For a perfect party food, you can easily lose the skewers and make these into bite-size pieces. Just plan to make more batter.

Corn Dogs were one of our favorite snack foods at *fairs and events*. Who can resist that aroma or, for that matter, eating *food on a stick?* Incredibly, even this can be recreated nutritiously! The secret ingredient? The health-promoting spice turmeric, which gives the batter its distinctive yellow color. Of course, while you have your fryer out, we suggest pairing these with *Potato Crisps* (page 198).

"CORN" DOGS

1. In a bowl, sift together ½ cup of the tapioca flour, the almond flour, arrowroot powder, turmeric, and salt.

2. In a separate mixing bowl, whisk the egg yolks together until they begin to lighten slightly. Then, add the dry ingredients until well combined. The mixture will be very dry and crumbly.

3. Slowly pour the water into the dry mixture, whisking to avoid lumps. Once the batter is wet and smooth, set aside.

4. In a separate bowl, add the remaining ¼ cup tapioca flour, and set it aside.

5. Insert a skewer ¾ of the way into the end of each hot dog.

6. Pat the tapioca flour onto the surface of each hot dog, and wipe off the excess flour with a towel. If you do not adequately remove the extra flour, the batter will slide off of the hot dog.

7. Hold the skewer downward, and spoon the batter evenly from the base (where the skewer is sticking out) to ensure that a thick, even layer drips down over the entire hot dog.

8. Measure the skewers and pan before you drop in the "corn" dogs, cutting off the tips of the skewer where necessary so that the "corn" dog is completely immersed within the fryer.

9. Gently place the "corn" dogs into the 350°F oil, making sure that they do not touch each other (we recommend only 1 or 2 at the same time). If using an electric fryer, do not use the basket because the batter will stick to it.

10. Flip the dogs after 2-3 minutes, using a set of tongs to turn them by the skewer end. The batter should be evenly cooked all over.

11. When the "corn" dogs turn golden brown, after 6-8 minutes, move them to a towel-lined plate or rack, and allow them to cool for 10 minutes before eating. Don't skip this step! Allowing the towel to absorb the excess fat is what will help crisp the coating of the "corn" dogs!

DIFFICULTY
Intermediate

TIME to TABLE
Under 30 minutes

SERVES
4-6

PREHEAT
Frying oil to 350°F

EQUIPMENT
Heavy-bottomed pot or electric fryer

INGREDIENTS

PORK AND BATTER

½ cup tapioca flour

2 tablespoons arrowroot powder

½ teaspoon salt

¼ teaspoon white pepper

2 egg yolks

½ cup water

2 teaspoons coconut aminos or wheat-free tamari

2 pounds pork shoulder, cut into ½-inch cubes

Lard (page 62) for frying

SWEET & SOUR SAUCE

¼ cup apple cider vinegar

¼ cup pineapple juice

2 tablespoons honey

2 tablespoons coconut aminos or wheat-free tamari

1 tablespoon arrowroot powder

1 tablespoon tomato paste

1 green bell pepper, sliced into 1-inch squares

½ cup pineapple chunks

½ cup carrots, sliced on the bias into ½-inch rounds

Unfortunately, most Chinese takeout menu items are coated in soy sauce (with wheat), deep fried in oxidized vegetable oil, colored with red dye no. 40, and sweetened with a whole lot of sugar. We all know that doesn't stop it from being delicious! *The good news* is this recreation is so amazingly spot-on, you'll be able to *impress your family* and friends at the next movie night by making takeout at home!

SWEET & SOUR PORK

1. In a bowl, sift together the tapioca flour, arrowroot powder, salt, and white pepper.

2. In a separate mixing bowl, whisk the egg yolks together until they begin to lighten slightly. Then, add the dry ingredients, whisking until well combined. The mixture will be very dry and crumbly.

3. Slowly pour the water and coconut aminos into the dry mixture, whisking to avoid lumps. Once the batter is wet and smooth, set aside.

4. Dry the pork cubes very well, which will allow the batter to adhere to them better. Coat each pork cube by immersing it completely in the batter.

5. In a heavy-bottomed pot (or electric fryer), heat 2-3 cups of rendered Lard to 350°F. Make sure that the pork "nuggets" are completely submerged in the fat while cooking.

6. Fry the pork in small batches for about 3 minutes. The amount of pork will depend on the size of your pan or fryer, but make sure that the pieces do not touch one another and that the heat doesn't drop (which will happen if you put too many cold pieces of meat in the pan at once). If you use a deep fryer, do not use the basket, as the pieces will stick to it.

7. Once the pieces rise to the top and are a golden brown color, remove them from the heat, and allow them to rest on a towel-covered plate or rack. Don't skip this step! Allowing the towel to absorb the excess fat is what will help crisp the coating of the fried pork.

8. Meanwhile, in a small saucepan, make the sauce by whisking together the apple cider vinegar, pineapple juice, honey, coconut aminos, and arrowroot powder over medium heat. Simmer for 5 minutes. Then, whisk in the tomato paste.

9. Add the bell pepper, pineapple chunks, and carrots. Simmer the sauce for another 10 minutes. Remove it from the heat, and allow it to sit and thicken for at least 10 minutes while you finish frying the pork.

10. To serve, allow people to pour the sauce over the pork at the table. Pouring the sauce too early will make the pork pieces become prematurely soggy. For leftovers, however, this is enjoyable, as the coating will soak up the delicious sauce, especially when combined with our Pork Fried Cauliflower Rice (page 206)!

After you've rendered a pot of back fat into lard, what do you do with all the extra meat pieces? Why not make them into lardons? The French love these *little bits of heaven*, but they haven't caught on as much in America. This recipe should help change that. Simply put, lardons are small pieces of meaty fat that are crisped up to create a porky garnish or accent for texture in salads or omelets or soup. We even use them on our *Dutch Apple Pie* (page 274)!

DIFFICULTY
Basic

TIME TO TABLE
Less than 30 minutes

YIELD
Makes about a cup

INGREDIENTS
Remaining meat bits left over after rendering lard (page 62)

CRISPY LARDONS

1. In a large skillet, spread out the remaining bits of ground meat and chunks of fat into a single layer over medium-low heat (after removing most of the fat from the rendered lard).

2. As the meat begins to fry, more lard will render off. Pour off the extra fat, and stir. You'll likely need to do this every couple of minutes. Save this fat in a separate container, as it will have a more distinctly porky and sometimes smoky taste. If it turns brown after it has solidified, like the picture at the top of page 63, discard it; do not use it for cooking.

3. When the fat pieces have melted off and all that's left are meaty chunks that have turned a light to medium brown color (per your preference), they are ready. Drain them again, and remove them from the heat. If they turn dark brown, they will begin to taste bitter and burnt.

4. With a slotted spoon, transfer the browned fat to a towel-lined plate or rack, and allow to drain, dry, and crisp for 10 minutes.

5. Refrigerate in an airtight container, and add it to soups, salads, and eggs often!

Note: **Though we recommend using the remains of the fat you rendered into lard, any small pieces of pork fat will do—from pork belly, ham or roast trimmings, or even bacon.**

Known for their delicious flavor, crunchy texture, and collagen-rich, *low-carb snack appeal*, pork rinds have been a staple in American diets for some time. Problem is, when you consume the skin and fat of an animal that wasn't raised in a healthful way, you're eating a concentrated form of the toxins stored in their fat and organs (the skin, after all, is the largest organ in the body). This recipe, though somewhat complicated, gives you the same light, puffy texture of the bagged brands you've come to love. Known also as chicharones and pork rinds, we went with *Cracklin'* because of how much we enjoy the "crackling" sounds that continues long after the rinds have been removed from the hot fat. You'll marvel at how the (somewhat tedious) process turns squishy skin into *an airy, tasty treat!*

CURRIED CRACKLIN'S

DIFFICULTY
Advanced

TIME to TABLE
6-12 hours

SERVES
8-12

PREHEAT
Frying oil to 375°F

EQUIPMENT
Dehydrator (optional), electric fryer or heavy-bottomed pot

INGREDIENTS

2 pounds pork skin

Lard for frying (page 62)

2 tablespoons yellow curry powder (optional)

2 tablespoons salt

1. Slice the pork skin into 1-inch by 2-inch sections, or ask your processor or butcher to do this for you when ordering (this is usually done without an extra charge).

2. In a large saucepan, boil water. Submerge the pork skins (thawed or fresh) in the boiling water for 10 minutes, and remove them from the water. Place them on a drying rack, and cover them with towels to dry for 1 hour.

3. Once the pork skins are dry, dehydrate them at 165°F for about 6 hours, flipping them about halfway through. Alternatively, lay them out on a baking sheet, and bake them on the lowest oven temperature for about 10 hours, also flipping halfway through. After dehydrating, the skins will be very hard and can sit at room temperature for a few days until you are ready to finish them by frying. Dogs also love to chew on them at this point!

4. When ready, bring the Lard to 375°F in a heavy-bottomed pot or electric fryer. Submerge the pork skin pieces completely in the melted Lard. Fry them for about 6 minutes or until they are puffed and crispy. Do not overcrowd the frying space, and work in batches, as the pieces will puff up to double their original size.

5. If you're going to snack on these, we recommend that you sprinkle them with curry powder and salt or your favorite spice flavors. It will remove a bit of the pork flavor and remind you more of a flavored chip. However, for use in recipes, or if you particularly love the taste of pig skin, just sprinkle them with salt when warm.

Note: If you're stuck wondering what to do with pig ears, this is an excellent way to cook them. Pig ears are traditionally dehydrated for dog treats; it's the frying that inflates and creates the wonderfully crunchy (rather than leathery) texture!

Sweetbreads can refer to several glands. The most popular are the thymus (neck sweetbreads) or the pancreas (stomach sweetbreads). Often these parts are discarded, however they are among the most prized organs in the culinary arts. If you've paid for a whole pig, be sure to ask for these *incredibly nutrient-dense* parts; for anyone with a weakened thyroid or pancreatic function, those glands are exactly what your body needs more of!

The *best part* about sweetbreads is that they don't require the attention needed for cooking other, more delicate offal parts. It's virtually impossible to ruin sweetbreads by overcooking if properly prepared prior to cooking!

SWEETBREADS

DIFFICULTY
Advanced

TIME TO TABLE
More than 24 hours

SERVES
1

PREHEAT
Frying oil to 350°F

EQUIPMENT
Heavy-bottomed pot or electric fryer

INGREDIENTS

2 cups cold water

1 tablespoon lemon juice

2 neck sweetbreads

1 cup full-fat coconut milk

1 cup Pork Stock (page 66)

½ cup blanched almond flour

½ teaspoon salt

¼ teaspoon black pepper

1 teaspoon dried tarragon

¼ cup tapioca flour

¼ cup olive oil

Lard (page 62) for frying

Note: If you are getting a whole head in order to make Head Cheese (page 72), have your butcher remove the neck sweetbreads for you.

1. Pour the water into a bowl, and squeeze the lemon juice into the bowl.

2. Place the sweetbreads in the water, and allow them to soak overnight or at least 8 hours.

3. Remove the sweetbreads from the water, and place the meat in a small saucepan with the coconut milk and Pork Stock. Heat the pan on the stovetop over medium heat until the liquid comes to a gentle boil. Immediately remove the sweetbreads from the heat, strain them, and rinse them with cold water.

4. With a knife and your fingers, pull off the thin membrane that surrounds the sweetbreads, and remove any tougher pieces or veins.

5. Dry the sweetbreads by placing them between two layers of towels and flanking them between two plates. Refrigerate them in this squished position for 2 hours.

6. In a small bowl, combine the almond flour, salt, black pepper, and tarragon.

7. In 3 separate bowls, set up an assembly line. The first bowl will contain the tapioca flour, the second will contain the olive oil, and the third will contain the almond flour mixture.

8. Lightly dredge the sweetbreads in the tapioca flour, but be sure to remove as much excess as possible. Extra flour may cause the coating not to stick.

9. Dip the sweetbreads in the olive oil, and shake off the excess oil.

10. Coat the sweetbreads in the almond flour mixture. Be sure that all surfaces are covered.

11. Deep fry the sweetbreads for 5 minutes in 350°F Lard until the outside is golden brown. Remove them to a towel-lined plate or rack to dry.

Crispy fried plantain chips should be a staple in every house: they're affordable, filling, and hugely popular. They always *disappear in a flash!* Make a big batch and serve with guacamole, our *Spicy Horseradish Pepper Mayonnaise* (page 258), or your own favorite dip. Just about everything goes with plantains!

DIFFICULTY
Basic

TIME to TABLE
Less than 15 minutes

SERVES
4-6

PREHEAT
Frying oil to 350°F

EQUIPMENT
Electric fryer or heavy-bottomed pot

INGREDIENTS

4 green plantains, peeled

1 teaspoon salt

1 teaspoon ground cinnamon

½ teaspoon ground cumin

½ teaspoon ground coriander

Lard (page 62) for frying

PLANTAIN CHIPS

1. Slice the plantains on the bias to increase the surface area to about ⅓-inch thick slices.

2. In a small bowl, combine the salt, cinnamon, cumin, and coriander.

3. Add Lard to the pan or fryer and allow to come to 350°F.

4. Fry the plantain chips in small batches, being careful not to overcrowd them, which will reduce the cooking temperature of the Lard.

5. Remove the plantains from the pan when they turn golden brown, about 3 minutes. Allow them to dry and crisp on a towel-lined plate or rack. Between each batch, allow the Lard to return to temperature.

6. Before the plantains cool, sprinkle them with the salt mixture.

7. These chips are best served immediately, but they can be stored chilled for a week. They may lose their crispiness during this period, however. You can reheat them in a toaster oven or conventional oven before serving after they have been chilled.

What would being a couch potato be without potato chips? Not as much fun! We make ours with sweet potatoes, and naturally fry them in *homemade lard* rather than unstable canola oil. The result is *superior flavor and nutrition* with all the crunch and saltiness you crave from "junk" food.

DIFFICULTY
Basic

TIME to TABLE
Less than 15 minutes

SERVES
6-8

PREHEAT
Frying oil to 350°F

EQUIPMENT
Electric fryer or heavy-bottomed pot

INGREDIENTS

2 large sweet potatoes, about 2 pounds

1 tablespoon sea salt

2 teaspoons cinnamon

½ teaspoon mace

Lard (page 62) for frying

Note: Sweet potatoes come in all colors and varieties. We found these light yellow sweet potatoes at an Asian food market. They look enough like white potatoes to have fooled everyone except the most discerning of Paleo eaters at our house. The gorgeous purple Japanese sweet potato would be fun to fry too.

POTATO CRISPS

1. Peel and slice the sweet potatoes into very thin rounds, about 1/16 of an inch. We recommend using a mandolin if you have one, but careful work with a sharp knife works.

2. Dry the sweet potato rounds in between layers of towels, and allow them to sit and dry further for 10 minutes.

3. Add Lard to a heavy-bottomed pot or electric fryer and preheat to 350°F.

4. Fry the sweet potatoes until they turn golden but not brown, about 90 seconds. Do not overfill the fryer, and keep the crisps in a single layer.

5. Once golden, remove the crisps from the Lard, and allow them to dry and crisp on a towel-lined plate.

6. Sprinkle the crisps with the salt, cinnamon, and mace, and toss them while they are still hot. If you want a more traditional potato taste, skip the spices and just use sea salt.

Our area happens to have a large Peruvian population, and their delicious rotisserie chicken has become a staple at local restaurants. It's one of our family's *favorite meals* when we don't have time to cook. The boys particularly love the fried yuca the chicken is served with—they are the Peruvian answer to French fries. Unfortunately, most restaurants don't fry them in a stable cooking fat, so we set about recreating this crispy root vegetable our way. Dip them in our *Spicy Horseradish Pepper Mayonnaise* (page 258) for a perfectly yummy pairing!

DIFFICULTY
Intermediate

TIME to TABLE
Less than 30 minutes

SERVES
4-6

PREHEAT
Frying oil to 350°F

EQUIPMENT
Electric fryer or heavy-bottomed pot

INGREDIENTS
3 yuca, peeled, about 3 pounds

Sea salt

Lard (page 62) for frying

FRIED YUCA

1. Peel and slice the yucca in half lengthwise to remove the thick vein in the center of each. Create a spear shape by slicing them lengthwise in half and in half again before then slicing them horizontally into halves or thirds. The pieces should be 3 to 4 inches in length and about 1 inch thick.

2. Fill a pot with water, and add salt.

3. Boil the yuca in the salted water for 10 minutes until they are cooked through and easily pierced with a fork.

4. Dry the yuca spears by sandwiching them between layers of towels and allowing them to sit for at least 10 minutes.

5. In a heavy-bottomed pot or electric fryer, add Lard, and heat to 350°F.

6. Fry the yuca in the heated Lard for 3-5 minutes in a single layer, being careful not to overflow the fryer. After the yuca turns golden brown, remove the pieces to a towel-lined plate or rack. Immediately sprinkle them with sea salt while they are still warm.

7. These are best served immediately but can be stored chilled for a week. They may lose their crispiness, however. You can reheat them in a toaster oven or conventional oven before serving after they have been chilled.

There is nothing porky about vegetables. Unless, of course, you add a little pork flavor. We use lard and stock as well as bacon, pancetta, and sausage to turn normal vegetables into outrageously addictive side dishes that are so satisfying, they just might make you forget about the main course!

VEGGIES & SIDES

DIFFICULTY
Basic

TIME to TABLE
Under 30 minutes

SERVES
8-10

INGREDIENTS

2 cups Pork Stock (page 66)

1 pound pork jowl, thinly sliced on the bias (about 6 inches long and 2 inches wide)

2 pounds green papaya, julienned or shredded

2 carrots, julienned or shredded

⅓ cup lime juice

2 tablespoons fish sauce (Red Boat brand preferred)

1 shallot, minced

4 Thai bird chilies, seeded and minced

3 tablespoons granulated palm sugar

3 garlic cloves, minced

2 tablespoons cilantro, minced

½ cup roasted cashews, chopped (optional)

2 tablespoons fresh mint leaves, sliced (optional)

Note: Jowl, also called cheek, is a fatty, tender, and delicate cut prized in the culinary world. If you're unable to find this very affordable and delectable meat, other fatty and delicate cuts like belly work well in this recipe.

While driving through Pennsylvania, we happened into a small carryout *Laotian/Thai restaurant* whose owner was extremely accommodating and helped us navigate her wonderful and flavorful menu. Not knowing exactly what to expect, only that she was custom-making us a meal, we were thrilled when we walked out with a delicious salad made with green papaya and poached bacon that we had never even conceived of before. The dish was so wonderful we knew we needed to recreate it. We feel like the *magic of that night* is recaptured with the addition of stock poached jowl slices, which have a tender and fatty consistency just like bacon! This recipe happens to be the favorite of our photographer, Aimee, who had every single recipe in the book. So, although the ingredients may be harder to find, we all feel it's worth the effort. *Tip: Use a food processor or mandolin to julienne your vegetables and papaya!*

GREEN PAPAYA SALAD with POACHED JOWL

1. In a medium saucepan, heat the Pork Stock over medium heat until it boils.

2. Place several slices of the pork jowl into the Pork Stock, and cook it for 90 seconds. To maintain the boil and ensure that all pieces cook evenly, prepare this in batches. When each piece turns a light brown color, remove it from the heat with a slotted spoon, and set it aside to cool.

3. Once the meat has rested, slice the pieces of jowl further into ¼-½ inch-thick slices, resembling the same julienned shape as the vegetables.

4. In a serving bowl, toss the pork, papaya, carrots, lime juice, fish sauce, shallot, chilies, sugar, garlic, and cilantro together until thoroughly combined. The salad is best made a few hours ahead of time so that the flavors can meld together. This is a large quantity, but we find leftovers even better than the day we served it!

5. Prior to serving, top the salad with optional chopped nuts and fresh mint.

Cauliflower rice can be tricky. You *should* end up with a *tasty, grain-free pseudo-carb* that can work as a base for meats, but more often than not you end up with soggy mush. With this recipe, we figured out a way to *retain a rice-like texture*. This dish works with so many dishes—it's as adaptable as white rice!

DIFFICULTY
Intermediate

TIME TO TABLE
Under 30 minutes

SERVES
4-6

EQUIPMENT
Wok or large skillet; food processor; microwave

INGREDIENTS

1 head cauliflower (about 4 cups)

2 teaspoons salt

2 tablespoons Lard (page 62)

¾ pound dark pork meat (leftover pork chop and shoulder are great here)

½ cup yellow onion, diced

½ cup carrots, diced

½ cup mushrooms (shiitake or oyster preferred), diced

2 cloves garlic, minced

2 eggs, whisked

1 green onion, sliced

1½ tablespoons fish sauce (Red Boat brand preferred)

1½ tablespoons coconut aminos or wheat-free tamari

¼ teaspoon white pepper

1 teaspoon sesame oil

1 tablespoon sesame seeds

PORK FRIED CAULIFLOWER RICE

1. Chop the cauliflower into small pieces, and place the florets in a food processor. Pulse until the cauliflower is rice-sized, about 8 times.

2. Microwave the cauliflower rice for 3 minutes. Alternatively, add salt to the cauliflower, stir, and allow it to rest for 15 minutes.

3. Meanwhile, add the Lard to a wok or large skillet, and brown the diced pork over medium-high heat if not already cooked.

4. Press the water out of the cauliflower with cheesecloth or a strainer.

5. Add the onion, carrots, mushrooms, garlic, and cauliflower to the wok or skillet. Sauté until the onion is translucent but not browned.

6. Create a void in the center of the skillet by pushing the vegetables to the edges. Pour the whisked eggs into the center of the pan. Scramble the eggs by whisking them constantly in the center. When the eggs have broken into tiny pieces and cooked but not browned, incorporate the vegetables back into the center with the eggs.

7. Add the green onion, fish sauce, coconut aminos, and white pepper to the pan. Reduce the heat to medium, and toss the ingredients in the skillet to coat with the liquid. Continue to sauté for another 5 minutes.

8. Remove the pan from the heat, and add the sesame oil and sesame seeds to the dish. Toss to combine and serve.

DIFFICULTY
Basic

TIME to TABLE
Under 30 minutes

SERVES
4-6

PREHEAT
Pot of boiling water

EQUIPMENT
Steamer basket; food processor

INGREDIENTS

½ head cauliflower (about 2 cups)

¼ cup Lard (page 62)

1 teaspoon salt

1 teaspoon onion powder

½ teaspoon garlic powder

¼ teaspoon white pepper

In our house, this recipe gets a workout. Cauliflower is affordable, you can pair with almost anything, and you can get it on the table *in less than 15 minutes*. The lard adds the creamy texture we'd been missing since we quit dairy. We love it as a base for braised meats and stews, like the elegant *Porko Bucco* (page 134) pictured. And we definitely recommend topping it with our *Liver Gravy* (page 252).

MASHED CAULIFLOWER

1. Chop the cauliflower into evenly sized florets, and place them in a steamer basket. Steam over boiling water for about 10 minutes or until they are easily pierced with a fork.

2. Transfer the softened cauliflower to a food processor and purée until smooth.

3. Add the Lard, salt, onion powder, garlic powder, and white pepper to the food processor, and pulse again. The end result should be completely smooth, and all of the Lard should be melted and fully incorporated into the cauliflower.

Note: If you're not serving your Mashed Cauliflower under another dish or paired with Liver Gravy (page 252), we suggest adding fresh herbs along with other spices. Flat leaf parsley, thyme, and rosemary are fantastic additions!

Butternut squash is an oblong squash with a bulbous end that tends to arrive in stores in the late fall and sticks around all winter. Our kids love it, so we often mash it with cinnamon, like a sweet potato. But this version is more elegant and almost dessert-like. We like it with eggs and *Maple Sage Breakfast Sausage Links* (page 78) or paired with a slow-roasted meat, like *Braised Neck Roast* (page 130). It is a comfort food that pleases almost any palate!

DIFFICULTY
Basic

TIME to TABLE
30-60 minutes

SERVES
4-6

PREHEAT
Oven to 350°F

INGREDIENTS

1 medium butternut squash, about 2 pounds

8 fresh sage leaves

2 tablespoons maple syrup

2 tablespoons Lard (page 62), melted

1 teaspoon salt

¼ teaspoon black pepper

MAPLE SAGE ROASTED BUTTERNUT SQUASH

1. Cut off each end of the squash, peel it, and slice it in half. Using a spoon, scoop out the seeds. Butternut squash is very hard, like a pumpkin. A good quality vegetable peeler or paring knife works best for removing the tough skin.

2. Dice the squash to ¼-½-inch cubes, and spread the pieces on a baking sheet.

3. Chiffonade* the sage leaves, and toss with the squash, maple syrup, Lard, salt, and black pepper.

4. Roast the squash in the oven for 30 minutes at 350°F, tossing halfway through. When done, the cubes will be soft and easily pierced with a fork with a slight caramelization to some of the edges and sides.

*Note: Chiffonade is just a fancy way of describing the technique of stacking the herb leaves on top of each other, rolling them together tightly, then slicing them into thin ribbons. It prevents fresh herbs from bruising when you cut them, and is our recommendation for cutting all fresh herb leaves.

DIFFICULTY
Basic

TIME to TABLE
1-2 hours

SERVES
4-6

INGREDIENTS

1 jicama, skin removed and cut into 1-inch cubes

1 celeriac, skin removed and cut into 1-inch cubes

½ cup Pancetta (page 70), diced

4 eggs, hard-boiled and diced

½ cup Baconnaise (page 256)

1 tablespoon Dijon mustard

1 teaspoon dried tarragon

1 teaspoon smoked paprika

Note: Jicama is a very dense tuber that is often eaten raw. Boiling takes a long time to make it soft enough to eat in the salad. Celeriac, also known as celery root, is a softer root that brings out the fresh and spicy flavor similar to celery, but with a completely unique texture.

No pork cookbook is complete without *barbeque*. And no matter how delicious your barbeque, guests are going to be looking for the potato salad. Instead of white potatoes, we use a few starchy vegetables, each with their *own unique taste*.

We've all got a family member or friend who likes to rib us about our crazy Paleo diet. For the ones in your life, serve this up with our *Slow Roasted Shoulder* (page 140); we predict the ribbing will stop. Anyone we've served our Faux-Tato Salad to couldn't get enough of it.

FAUX-TATO SALAD

1. Fill a large pot with water, and bring it to a boil.

2. Add the jicama cubes, and boil for 45 minutes, adding the celeriac in the last 10 minutes. You should be able to pierce all pieces through with a fork. The jicama will have more of a bite to it and will be more difficult to pierce, but it should still be tender once cooked through.

3. In a small separate pan over medium heat, fry the Pancetta until it is crispy, about 6 minutes.

4. In a large mixing bowl, combine the jicama, celeriac, Pancetta, hard-boiled eggs, Baconnaise, Dijon mustard, tarragon, and smoked paprika. Toss to combine, and serve warm; or, chill and let the flavors combine up to a couple days before serving.

DIFFICULTY
Intermediate

TIME to TABLE
1-2 hours

SERVES
8-10

PREHEAT
Oven to 375°F

INGREDIENTS

4 sweet potatoes, peeled and quartered

1 tablespoon coconut oil, melted

2 bananas, in peel

1 cup crushed pineapple, juice drained

¼ cup Lard (page 62), melted

¾ teaspoon ground allspice

½ teaspoon mace

½ cup pecans, chopped

¼ cup Crispy Lardons (page 190)

2 tablespoons palm, maple, or date granulated sugar

1 teaspoon cinnamon

Years ago we found a recipe for a sweet potato casserole that included roasted bananas. Having never been fans of the sickly sweet marshmallow-topped sweet potato casseroles served at most holiday parties, we adapted the recipe and made it our own. It's now a *Thanksgiving menu staple*, and we get a lot of requests for it from non-Paleo family members throughout the holidays. Grandchildren and grandparents alike lick their plates clean!

SWEET POTATO CASSEROLE

1. Place the sweet potatoes on a lined baking sheet, toss them with the melted coconut oil, and roast them at 375°F for 15 minutes.

2. Flip the sweet potatoes, and place the whole bananas on the baking sheet. Bake for another 15 minutes.

3. Let the sweet potatoes and bananas cool a bit, and then peel the bananas.

4. Mash or purée the sweet potatoes and roasted bananas together.

5. Add the crushed pineapple, Lard, allspice, and mace, and mix or mash until all ingredients are combined. The Lard should melt entirely and be thoroughly incorporated.

6. In a small bowl, stir together the pecans, Crispy Lardons, sugar, and cinnamon.

7. Sprinkle the pecan topping onto the top of the sweet potato casserole. Bake at 350°F for 30 minutes.

Note: Roasting bananas in their own peel enhances and sweetens their natural flavors.

DIFFICULTY
Basic

TIME to TABLE
Less than 90 minutes

SERVES
4-6

PREHEAT
Pot of boiling water

INGREDIENTS

1 pound green beans, ends removed

2 tablespoons Lard (page 62)

1 cup porcini (baby bella) mushrooms, diced

2 shallots, diced

2 garlic cloves, minced

1 pound Pancetta (page 70), diced

½ teaspoon salt

¼ teaspoon white pepper

½ teaspoon red pepper flakes (optional)

Note: **You may be asking yourself,** *But this is a bean! Isn't that a legume? How is this Paleo?*

The consensus on green beans is that they're more pod than bean. They can also be eaten fresh, which makes them more digestible than other legumes. If you find they don't agree with you, then definitely avoid them.

Growing up, Stacy often helped her mother prepare dinner. She'd sit at the kitchen table snapping green beans as her mom told stories about her own mother's southern cooking; green beans and ham cooked in bacon fat was one of the family favorites. These beans pair beautifully with our *Perfect Pork Chops* (page 170) or with Asian dishes, like our *Asian Short Ribs* (page 104).

SAUTÉED GREEN BEANS

1. Steam or boil the green beans until tender, about 3 minutes.

2. Strain the green beans through a colander, and rinse them with cold water. Set them aside.

3. In a large skillet, melt the Lard over medium heat.

4. Add the mushrooms, shallots, garlic, and Pancetta to the skillet, and sauté for 6 minutes, stirring occasionally.

5. Add the green beans, salt, white pepper, and red pepper flakes to the skillet, and stir to combine. Continue to cook another 10 minutes, stirring occasionally. Serve warm.

One of the things we missed after giving up grains was biscuits; we had visions of hot, pop n' fresh biscuits *dancing in our heads!* We went for years without them, until we hit upon this recipe, which takes advantage of the versatility of lard. You can actually roll this dough out and use a biscuit cutter! These are integral to our *Piggie Pot Pie* (page 150), or you can slather them with *Sausage Mushroom & Gravy* (page 254) for the ultimate brunch feast. The flaky biscuits are perfect for sopping up wet gravy; our mouths are watering just thinking about them!

DIFFICULTY
Intermediate

TIME TO TABLE
30-60 minutes

YIELD
Makes 6 thick biscuits

PREHEAT
Over to 450°F

EQUIPMENT
Electric mixer

INGREDIENTS
½ cup Lard (page 62), cold

1½ cups blanched almond flour

½ cup tapioca flour

⅓ cup coconut flour

1½ teaspoon cream of tartar

2½ teaspoons baking soda

¾ teaspoon salt

⅔ cup full-fat coconut milk

1 egg white

HOMESTYLE BISCUITS

1. Form a square-shaped mound with the Lard. Place it on wax paper, and put it in the freezer for at least 15 minutes to chill.

2. While waiting, in a large mixing bowl, sift the almond flour, tapioca flour, coconut flour, cream of tartar, baking soda, and salt.

3. Dice the very cold Lard into small pieces. Try not to touch it so that it doesn't warm from your hands. If the Lard is not still cold, put it back in the freezer for a few minutes after it has been diced.

4. Cut the Lard into the dry ingredients with a pastry cutter or fork until crumbly.

5. Once the mixture sticks together, add the coconut milk, and mix the ingredients with a spatula until smooth and completely wet.

6. In a separate small bowl, whip the egg white until soft peaks form. For ease, use your hand mixer or stand mixer.

7. Fold the egg whites into the batter with a spatula until well combined.

8. Form the biscuits by hand into 2½ x ½-inch diameter rounds. If perfect biscuits are desired, flour the surface and rolling pin lightly with tapioca flour, and use a round biscuit cutter.

9. Bake the biscuits on a lined baking sheet at 450°F for 12 minutes.

DIFFICULTY
Basic

TIME to TABLE
Under 30 minutes

SERVES
4-6

EQUIPMENT
Food processor or masher

INGREDIENTS

6 medium carrots, about 1 pound, ends removed, peeled, and cut into 2-inch chunks

2 tablespoons Lard (page 62)

2 tablespoons full-fat coconut milk

1 tablespoon fresh rosemary, chopped

1 teaspoon fresh thyme, chopped

1 teaspoon salt

1 teaspoon black pepper

Carrots are one of our *favorite vegetables*. They are not generally considered an elegant vegetable, but in this dish, rich with flavor, they couldn't be classier. It's also *super simple and quick*. We serve it almost every week, and if there are any leftovers, the kids arm wrestle for them at breakfast. See how savory herbs rejuvenate the humble carrot; this is an absolute favorite among recipe testers!

ROSEMARY CARROT MASH

1. Steam or boil the carrots until they are tender when pierced with a fork, about 10 minutes.

2. Strain the carrots, and transfer them to a food processor or bowl for mashing. Pulse 5 times for 2 seconds or mash the carrots to a chunky consistency.

3. Add the Lard, coconut milk, rosemary, thyme, salt, and black pepper, and pulse or mash until all ingredients are combined thoroughly and all of the Lard has melted. Serve warm.

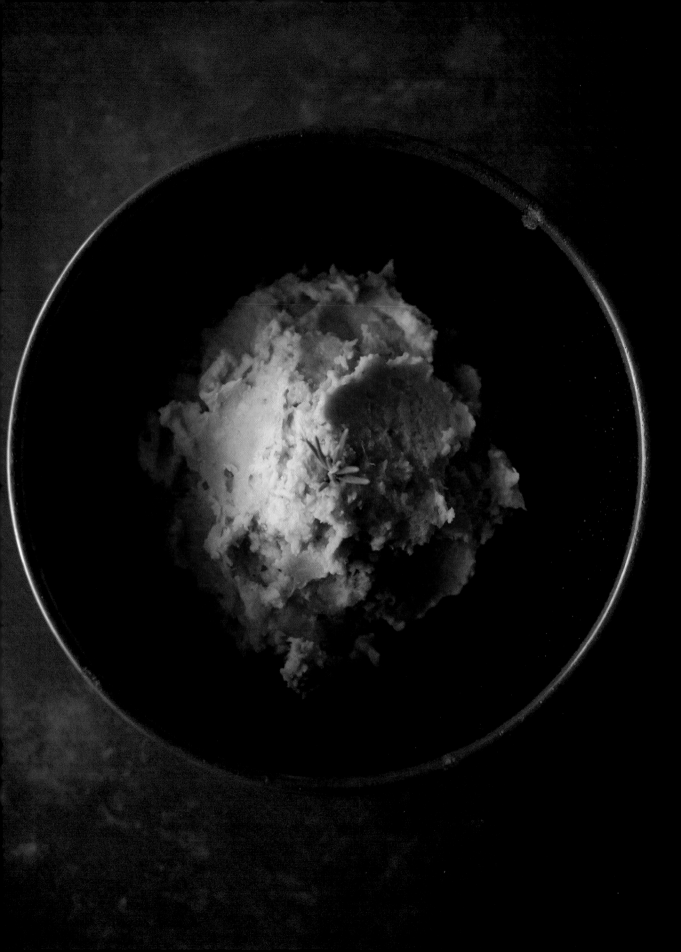

The rich herbs of fall enhance the natural, earthy sweetness of sweet potatoes in these Savory Drop Biscuits. They'll be a hit with your Thanksgiving turkey or with your weekday *Bacon Chicken* (page 176). On a cold winter day, we like to slather them with *Lard Butter* (page 246) and serve with soups and stews. Why not *warm your belly and you heart* with these addictive little wonders?

DIFFICULTY
Basic

TIME TO TABLE
Under 30 minutes

YIELD
Makes 8 biscuits

PREHEAT
Oven to 350°F

EQUIPMENT
Food processor

INGREDIENTS

1 cup sweet potato, peeled and cubed

¼ cup Lard (page 62)

2 eggs

2 teaspoons fresh rosemary

2 teaspoons fresh sage

1 teaspoon fresh thyme

1 teaspoon fresh tarragon

2 cups blanched almond flour

½ teaspoon salt

1 teaspoon baking soda

½ teaspoon cream of tartar

SWEET POTATO DROP BISCUITS

1. Boil or steam the sweet potato cubes until tender and easily pierced with a fork, about 10 minutes. Strain them, and run them under cool water.

2. In a food processor, purée the sweet potato cubes with the Lard, eggs, rosemary, sage, thyme, and tarragon until smooth.

3. Add the almond flour, salt, baking soda, and cream of tartar, and pulse until the ingredients are fully incorporated. The dough should be firm and pliable but not quite dry enough to roll out. If your dough is wetter than this, add additional almond flour to the dough as needed, and pulse until the consistency is right.

4. Form the dough by hand into 8 biscuits of about 2½ inches in diameter and place on a greased or parchment-lined baking sheet.

5. Bake the biscuits at 350°F for 15-18 minutes until the top begins to brown and the biscuits are almost firm all the way to the center.

Matt's mother makes *an amazing parsnip purée* during the holidays. When we asked her for her secret to this luscious dish, we were surprised to hear it was a sweet and earthy turnip! When we're tired of cauliflower or sweet potatoes, this is our go-to mash. The addition of lard and stock make it rich and creamy, perfect for pairing with the *Ham Pot Roast* (page 128). Or you can serve it with *Bacon Chicken* (page 176) and *Liver Gravy* (page 252) as a great sub for fried chicken, mashed potatoes, and flour-based gravy!

DIFFICULTY
Basic

TIME to TABLE
Under 30 minutes

SERVES
4-6

EQUIPMENT
Food processor

INGREDIENTS

1 pound turnips, peeled and cubed into 1-inch pieces

1 pound parsnips, peeled and cubed into 1-inch pieces

⅓ cup Lard (page 62)

⅓ cup Pork Stock (page 66)

Salt and pepper to taste

Fresh herbs of your choice for garnish (optional)

TURNIP AND PARSNIP PUREE

1. Steam or boil the turnips and parsnips until they are tender when pierced with a fork, about 10 minutes.

2. Remove the vegetables from the heat, and run them under cool water.

3. Add the parsnips, turnips, Lard, Pork Stock, salt, and pepper to a food processor, and purée until smooth.

4. Top the purée with the fresh herbs of your choice or another dollop of Lard.

DIFFICULTY
Basic

TIME to TABLE
30-60 minutes

SERVES
4-6

PREHEAT
Oven to 350°F

INGREDIENTS

1 pound Brussels sprouts

1 tablespoon Lard (page 62), or bacon fat, melted

½ pound Bacon (page 68), cut into ¼-inch strips

½ cup walnuts, chopped and toasted

½ cup roasted chestnuts, diced

Note: Roasted chestnuts are a great addition to lots of dishes. They're higher in starch and lower in calories than other nuts, and their softer consistency works as a replacement for grain. They are also a great source of Vitamin C, fiber, and folate. Buy a large bag of pre-prepared roasted chestnuts online and keep them on hand to use as needed.

Whoever put Brussels sprouts on the yucky veggie list was dead wrong. Sure, they can be soggy and bitter in the wrong hands. But when prepared correctly, these *health-filled baby cabbages* can be one of the most delicious vegetables around—especially when paired with bacon (turns out they were made for each other). This salad is extremely popular whenever we serve it at parties; it's great with our *Smoked Spare Ribs* (page 106), too. One taste and we think you'll agree that Brussels sprouts are awesome!

SHREDDED BRUSSELS SPROUT SALAD

1. With a grater or food processor with a grating attachment, shred the Brussels sprouts.

2. Toss the Brussels sprouts with the Lard and bacon so that every piece is coated with the Lard.

3. Place the Brussels sprouts and bacon on a baking sheet in one layer. Bake at 350°F for 35 minutes.

4. Transfer the salad to a large bowl, and toss it with the walnuts and chestnuts.

DIFFICULTY
Basic

TIME TO TABLE
Under 30 minutes

SERVES
4-6

INGREDIENTS

½ head cabbage, about ¾ pound

2 tablespoons bacon grease or Lard (page 62)

Salt and pepper to taste

If you'd told us five years ago that cabbage would be our favorite vegetable, we'd have laughed in your face. Then we started sautéing it in lard and bacon grease, and now we *eat it almost every day*. The kids beg for it at every meal! Not only is cabbage very affordable, it can be paired with just about anything. It's an excellent replacement for noodles under our *Italian Tomato Pork Chops* (page 164), or with eggs and herbs for breakfast. Soon cabbage will be your favorite vegetable, too!

SAUTÉED CABBAGE

1. Slice the cabbage into ¼-inch strips. We find it best to quarter the cabbage and slice it thin along the length. You won't need to chop further, as the noodle-like ribbons will naturally separate.

2. In a large skillet, melt the bacon grease or Lard over medium heat.

3. Add the cabbage, and cook, tossing and stirring regularly, until it has begun to soften and brown, about 10 minutes.

4. Add salt and pepper to taste before serving.

Note: For storing cabbage you've already cut into (or any vegetable, for that matter), place the head in an airtight container with a slice of lemon or juiced lemon rind. The citric acid will slow down the browning process and prevent the cabbage from becoming tough.

Balsamic vinegar is a new favorite ingredient for us. We use it on salads, desserts, and especially vegetables. Coating summer squash in this *sweet and tangy vinegar* improves the vegetable's flavor dramatically. We pair this summer staple with our *50/50 Burgers, Take 2* (page 100).

DIFFICULTY
Basic

TIME to TABLE
Under 30 minutes

SERVES
4

INGREDIENTS

1 medium zucchini

1 medium yellow squash

1 yellow onion

2 tablespoons Lard (page 62)

2 tablespoons balsamic vinegar

½ teaspoon salt

⅛ teaspoon black pepper

BALSAMIC SUMMER SQUASH

1. Cut the zucchini, yellow squash, and onion into the same size and shape. The squash should be in ¼-inch rounds, and the onion should be sliced into ¼-inch rounds and halved for a crescent-like shape.

2. In a medium skillet, melt the Lard over medium heat. Add the onion and squash, and cook them until they are softened, about 6 minutes.

3. Add the balsamic vinegar, salt, and black pepper, and stir until the vegetables are coated.

4. Simmer for 5 minutes until well combined. Serve warm.

Note: If you find that you enjoy balsamic, look for specialty vinegars at gourmet stores. It might be a little pricey, but since you don't need much of it, the bottles last a long time. Use espresso balsamic as a meat marinade, or a smoked balsamic for drizzling over fresh tomatoes in the summer.

DIFFICULTY
Advanced

TIME to TABLE
30-60 minutes

SERVES
6-8

PREHEAT
Oven to 425°F

EQUIPMENT
Soufflé dish; electric mixer

INGREDIENTS

1 tablespoon Lard (page 62)

2 tablespoons tapioca flour

3 slices Bacon (page 68), cut into ½-inch squares

1 yellow onion, finely diced

2 cups almond milk (unsweetened)

4 tablespoons arrowroot powder

6 eggs, separated into 5 yolks and 6 whites

1½ teaspoons salt

1 teaspoon black pepper

2 cups baby spinach leaves, lightly packed

The word soufflé can send some cooking neophytes into a panic. It has a reputation for being one of those dishes only a seasoned chef can pull off. Well, *here's a little secret:* making a soufflé is not as hard as you think. As long as you don't pop the air bubbles with careless handling and provide a stable and calm environment once you remove it from the oven, you will produce a soufflé *as light and fluffy as the ones you see in magazines.* And here's the best part—even if it falls it will still taste great!

SPINACH & BACON SOUFFLÉ

1. Fill a shallow baking dish (large enough to hold your soufflé dish) ½ inch deep in water, and put it into the oven while it preheats.

2. Rub the Lard over the inside of the soufflé dish, as well as on a sheet of aluminum foil, folded lengthwise (long enough to wrap around the dish).

3. Coat the dish and foil with the tapioca flour, and shake off any excess. Wrap the aluminum foil around the dish, and fold it together to secure it. This serves as a "collar" for the dish to support the soufflé as it rises.

4. In a skillet over medium heat, cook the bacon and onion for 8 minutes or until the bacon is crispy and the onion is soft. Set the bacon and onion aside on a towel to drain the fat.

5. In a separate large saucepan, heat the almond milk until it just starts to bubble.

6. Add the arrowroot powder and whisk for 2 minutes to thicken the almond milk. Remove it from the heat.

7. Add the bacon and onions to the simmering milk, and stir.

8. In a separate bowl, beat the egg yolks along with the salt and pepper.

9. Pour about ⅓ of the milk mixture into the egg yolks, and whisk to combine. This tempers the egg yolks so they do not scramble.

10. Pour the yolks back into the rest of the milk, and whisk to fully combine.

11. Beat the egg whites until stiff peaks form. Fold them into the yolk mixture, along with the spinach leaves.

12. Pour the mixture into the soufflé dish. Gently add the soufflé to the heated water bath baking dish, and return it to the oven to bake for 40 minutes at 425°F or until the top is golden brown and the soufflé has risen.

13. Gently remove the soufflé from the oven, and allow it to sit and settle in the water bath in a quiet, temperate environment for 10-15 minutes before removing it from the water bath or taking off the aluminum foil collar.

DIFFICULTY
Intermediate

TIME TO TABLE
Under 30 minutes

SERVES
4-6

PREHEAT
Oven to 350°F, pot of boiling water

EQUIPMENT
Vegetable peeler or mandolin

INGREDIENTS

1 pint cherry tomatoes

6 strips bacon, cut into 1-inch pieces

¼ cup fresh basil leaves, loosely packed

1 tablespoon Lard (page 62), melted

Salt and pepper to taste

3 medium zucchini squash, about 2 pounds

1 ripe avocado

Note: **There are special vegetable peelers designed for making vegetable "noodles" that you can find online and in stores relatively inexpensively. If you used to be a pasta lover, it's well worth the investment.**

Zucchini is *an amazing vegetable*. Somehow, it manages to absorb flavor and play well with almost anything you cook it with. It even serves as the perfect replacement for noodles! This dish employs zucchini noodles, the base of a dish *with the classic flavors of a BLT.*

ZUCCHINI PASTA WITH AVOCADO, ROASTED TOMATO & BACON

1. Bring a large pot with salted water to a boil, covered over high heat.

2. On a baking sheet, toss together the tomatoes, bacon, and basil with the Lard. Sprinkle with pepper, and toss again to fully coat.

3. Bake the tomatoes, bacon, and basil at 350°F for 20 minutes.

4. Meanwhile, cut off the ends of the zucchini, and cut them into ⅛ x ⅛-inch "noodles" down the length of each squash using a peeler, mandolin, knife, or spiral slicer.

5. Blanch the zucchini noodles for 2 minutes in the pot of boiling water. Then, immediately run cool water over the zucchini to stop cooking, and drain them thoroughly with a towel.

6. Once the tomato mixture is finished cooking toss it together with the zucchini noodles and avocado and serve. The avocado will mash a bit during the tossing, but this creates a creamy, wonderful consistency. Don't do this too early before serving, however, or the avocado will brown from the heat of the other ingredients.

DIFFICULTY
Basic

TIME TO TABLE
Under 30 minutes

SERVES
4

INGREDIENTS

12 mission figs, stems removed and quartered

½ pound prosciutto, cut in half

16 ounces field greens (including baby spinach, arugula, radicchio)

½ cup slivered almonds (optional)

½ cup shredded carrots (optional)

4-8 tablespoons balsamic vinegar (we recommend a fruit-based high quality one), divided

Note: We did not write a prosciutto recipe for this book since most people do not have the space at home to dedicate to curing a whole leg for several months. The good news, however, is that almost all prepared prosciuttos available at the deli counter contain just two ingredients: pork and salt. So enjoy the opportunity to buy something relatively safe at the store and use that ham for other recipes!

In our front yard is a very small fig tree that produces only enough figs to make this treat once a year—that is if the squirrels don't steal them first! Most people are only familiar with figs as a cookie filling or cheese pairing, but this *raindrop-shaped fruit* has a flavor that works *perfectly with meat*—particularly cured, salty pork.

PROSCIUTTO & FIG SALAD

1. Wrap each fig quarter with a prosciutto half. The meat will naturally stick to itself.

2. Toss together the greens, almonds, and carrots, and separate the salad equally into 4 separate bowls.

3. When ready to serve, pour 1-2 tablespoons of the balsamic vinegar on each bowl to coat. No oil is needed if you use good quality vinegar since the prosciutto adds a nice quality fat to the dish.

4. Nest the prosciutto-wrapped figs on top of each salad, and serve.

5. If you are taking this salad to a party or want to make it ahead of time, add the vinegar to the bottom of the bowl, and layer the ingredients on top. This will allow you to toss the salad later without the greens wilting. Keep the prosciutto-wrapped figs in a separate container until ready to serve so that they do not become unbound or bruised.

DIFFICULTY
Basic

TIME to TABLE
Under 30 minutes

SERVES
6-8

PREHEAT
Oven to 350°F

EQUIPMENT
Spice grinder or mortar and pestle

INGREDIENTS

2 star anise pods

1 cinnamon stick

6 peppercorns

1 teaspoon cumin seeds

1 teaspoon coriander seeds

½ teaspoon salt

4 ripe plantains, sliced on the bias into 1-inch chunks

3 tablespoons Lard (page 62)

What happens if a banana turns all its simple sugars into starch? You get its thicker cousin, the plantain. Plantains have a very unique flavor and a texture that *absorbs spices* incredibly well. Sautéing them in lard with Cuban flavors will open your eyes to their versatility. For the all-Cuban experience, pair these Plantains with our *Cuban Porchetta* (page 146).

CUBAN SPICED PLANTAINS

1. Grind the anise, cinnamon, peppercorns, cumin, coriander, and salt into a fine powder.

2. Toss the plantains with the spices until all pieces are coated.

3. In a large skillet (cast-iron preferred), melt the Lard over medium heat. Cook each side of the plantains for about 5 minutes. When cooked through, each side will have browned slightly to form a caramelization but will still be slightly soft in the center and not cooked through.

4. Transfer the skillet to the oven, and bake for 10 minutes at 350°F. Serve warm.

This is the kind of dish that recipe developers fantasize about—one of those let's-turn-whatever-we-have-in-the-fridge-into-a-great-meal challenges. Usually these dishes turn out fine, but occasionally you get something so transcendently good, you want to make it over and over—if you can remember how you made it to begin with!

Fortunately for you, we wrote this recipe down the first time. It's a *fantastic Thanksgiving side dish*, and also goes well with *Bacon Chicken* (page 176). It's extremely simple to put together, *and* you get a lot for leftovers.

PORK STUFFING CASSEROLE

DIFFICULTY
Basic

TIME to TABLE
30-60 minutes

SERVES
8-10 as a side dish

PREHEAT
Oven to 350°F

INGREDIENTS

1 pound ground pork

1 teaspoon fennel seeds

1 teaspoon fresh sage, chopped

½ teaspoon coriander, ground

2 teaspoons salt

½ teaspoon black pepper

1 tablespoon Lard (page 62)

1 cup carrots, diced

1 cup yellow onions, diced

1 cup celery, diced

1 cup mushrooms, diced

½ cup roasted chestnuts, diced

1 cup fresh cranberries

1 cup blanched almond flour

3 tablespoons Lard (page 62), cold

1 tablespoon fresh flat leaf Italian parsley, chopped

⅓ cup walnuts, chopped

1. In a medium-sized mixing bowl, combine the pork, fennel seeds, sage, coriander, salt, and black pepper by hand.

2. In a medium skillet, add the 1 tablespoon of Lard, and brown the meat mixture for about 8 minutes.

3. Drain the skillet, reserving the fat, and place the meat mixture in a 13 x 9-inch baking dish.

4. In the same skillet, using the reserved fat from the ground pork, cook the carrots, onions, celery, mushrooms, and chestnuts until soft, about 7 minutes.

5. Transfer the cooked vegetables to the baking dish, add the cranberries, and toss with the meat to combine.

6. In a small bowl, use a fork or pastry cutter to combine the almond flour, the 3 tablespoons of cold Lard, Italian parsley, and walnuts until crumbly.

7. Spread the crumbly mixture on top of the meat mixture.

8. Bake at 350°F for 30 minutes or until the top of the casserole begins to brown. Serve warm, and use an oven or toaster oven to reheat for best results.

Note: If you can't find fresh cranberries for this dish, use thawed, flash-frozen cranberries or diced green apple instead. Dried cranberries will be too sweet; it's the tartness that's needed to balance the sausage spices.

You've got the main courses and the side dishes, now all you have to do is sauce them! How could you serve a Smoked Pork Shoulder without some Carolina Style Barbecue Sauce? How could you eat Swedish Meatballs without Liver Gravy? And how will you live if you don't experience our favorite creation, Savory Bacon Jam?

SAUCES & DRESSINGS

There are no words for this recipe. Honestly, it's difficult to describe how cooking down bacon and onions with vinegar could create such a *luscious extravagance.* We keep this on hand for *pancakes* on Sunday morning (page 262), and enjoy it with our *Homestyle Biscuits* (page 218) and *Sweet Potato Drop Biscuits* (page 222). Pair it with green apple slices as a party appetizer; make a big batch and store it in mason jars in your refrigerator—just don't expect it to last long *before it's devoured!*

SAVORY BACON JAM

DIFFICULTY
Intermediate

TIME TO TABLE
3-6 hours

YIELD
Makes 2 pints of "jam"

EQUIPMENT
Dutch oven

INGREDIENTS

28 ounces (1¾ pounds) Bacon (page 68), sliced into ½-inch pieces

1 sweet white onion, minced

1 red onion, minced

5 garlic cloves, minced

¾ cup apple cider vinegar

¾ cup granulated maple or palm sugar

⅓ cup maple syrup

½ cup apple cider or juice

½ cup Pork Stock (page 66)

Note: This recipe makes a fantastic gift for special events and holidays—especially for people who need to be persuaded that Paleo foods are delicious and fun! We prefer to cook this in a Dutch oven, but it can be made in a crockpot. You will just need to cook it for a lot longer—6-10 hours on high with the lid off—and perhaps add a thickening starch like arrowroot powder.

1. In a Dutch oven on medium heat, cook the bacon pieces through. Then, set them aside on a towel to drain.

2. Pour off the excess bacon fat, except leave 2 tablespoons in the Dutch oven. Over medium heat, add the onion and garlic to the Dutch oven, and cook them until the onion is caramelized and softened to a light brown color, about 10 minutes.

3. Add the apple cider vinegar, sugar, maple syrup, apple cider, and Pork Stock to the Dutch oven. Deglaze the pan by scraping any remaining stuck bits off the bottom, and simmer for 5 minutes.

4. Return the bacon to the Dutch oven, and stir to combine.

5. Cook uncovered over medium heat 1-2 hours. The jam will be finished when the water is evaporated, and the consistency becomes thick and gelatinous, resulting in a dark brown caramel color.

6. Transfer the jam into mason jars or other airtight containers, chill to store, and serve with *everything!*

For those of you who are avoiding dairy, not having that stick of butter on the table to spread on your *Homestyle Biscuits* (page 218) or *Sweet Potato Drop Biscuits* (page 222) can be rough. Our solution was to simply whip lard into a *light and fluffy* butter-like consistency. To convert the porky flavor into the sweet creamy taste of butter, we added honey.

Don't just save this butter for biscuits: it definitely makes weeknight veggies a lot more exciting!

DIFFICULTY
Basic

TIME TO TABLE
Under 30 minutes

YIELD
Makes the equivalent of two sticks of butter

EQUIPMENT
Electric mixer

INGREDIENTS

1 cup Lard (page 62), soft but not melted

1 tablespoon honey

1 teaspoon kosher or sea salt

LARD BUTTER

1. In a stand mixer on high or a hand mixer and mixing bowl, whip the Lard until it is soft and light, about 5 minutes.

2. Add the honey and salt, and continue to whip to incorporate, another 1-2 minutes.

3. Store in a mason jar at room temperature for serving or chilled for long term storage.

There's something about the tangy, Carolina Style barbecue sauces, with their mix of vinegar and mustard, that we just can't get enough of. This sauce works beautifully with either our *Smoked Pulled Pork Shoulder* (page 92) or *Slow Roasted Shoulder* (page 140). It's a thinner style of barbecue sauce, so prepare for it to run all over your delicious pile of pork.

DIFFICULTY
Basic

TIME to TABLE
30-60 minutes

SERVES
8-10

INGREDIENTS
1 cup apple cider vinegar

½ cup Lard (page 62)

1 tablespoon brown mustard

1 tablespoon honey

1 teaspoon salt

1 teaspoon chili powder

½ teaspoon smoked paprika

¼ teaspoon cayenne pepper

¼ teaspoon black pepper

BBQ SAUCE, CAROLINA STYLE

1. In a small saucepan, whisk together the apple cider vinegar, Lard, mustard, and honey over medium-high heat. Continue stirring until the mustard and honey dissolve into the liquid.

2. When the mixture begins to boil, add the salt, chili powder, smoked paprika, cayenne pepper, and black pepper. Stir, and reduce the heat to medium-low.

3. Simmer for 10 minutes. Then, remove the pan from the heat, and allow the sauce to stand and thicken slightly as it cools at room temperature for 30 minutes.

4. The oil and vinegar will separate as it sits, but just like a salad dressing, give it a shake before serving.

Note: **For those unable to eat nightshades, substitute fresh herbs and lemon zest for the spices. You will have a uniquely autoimmune-friendly barbeque sauce!**

We've spent years testing Texas Style barbecue sauces, and this tomato-based version is our favorite by far. We keep the *spices mild*, but the depth of flavor is no less intense. It will perfectly compliment your *Picnic Ribs* (page 102)!

DIFFICULTY
Intermediate

TIME TO TABLE
30-60 minutes

SERVES
10-12

EQUIPMENT
Blender or immersion blender

INGREDIENTS
¼ cup Lard (page 62)

½ cup yellow onions, diced

3 cloves garlic, minced

½ cup celery, diced

1 cup natural ketchup

½ cup apple cider vinegar

1 cup water

¼ cup Worcestershire sauce

1 teaspoon black pepper

1 tablespoon chili powder

Note: **We have a recipe for homemade ketchup in our first cookbook, *Eat Like a Dinosaur*; but these days you can buy both ketchup and Worcestershire sauces made with natural and safe ingredients at any natural food store and virtually every grocery store. It definitely makes the prep for this sauce simpler.**

BBQ SAUCE, TEXAS STYLE

1. In a saucepan, melt the Lard over medium heat.

2. Add the onions, garlic, and celery, and cook until softened.

3. Add the ketchup, apple cider vinegar, water, Worcestershire sauce, and black pepper, and continue to simmer about 30 minutes.

4. In a small bowl, combine a few tablespoons of the sauce with the chili powder until smooth. Add this mixture to the rest of the sauce in the pan, and stir to combine.

5. Remove the sauce from the heat, and let it stand for an hour.

6. The slightly chunky sauce is nice as-is, but for a more traditional sauce, purée it in a blender or with an immersion blender.

7. This sauce is best served warm or at room temperature, but it stores well refrigerated in an airtight container.

DIFFICULTY
Intermediate

TIME TO TABLE
Less than 30 minutes

SERVES
4-6

EQUIPMENT
Food processor or blender

INGREDIENTS
1 pork liver, about ¾ pound
½ cup tapioca flour
½ teaspoon salt
⅛ teaspoon black pepper
1 tablespoon Lard (page 62)
2 cups Pork Stock (page 66)
¼ cup full-fat coconut milk

Liver is one of the *most nutritious foods* you can eat, full of nutrients not found in other muscle meats and foods: Vitamin A, Vitamin B12, and selenium. Lots of people don't like the taste or texture no matter how it's cooked, but it's worth finding a way to work it into your diet, and we think we've found it. This Liver Gravy gives you all the nutrition of liver without you having to actually chew it. When we serve it to family and friends with *Bacon Chicken* (page 176) and *Mashed Cauliflower* (page 208), it quickly disappears! Pair it with our *Shaken & Baked Pork Chops* (page 160) and you have Schnitzel. Our favorite way to eat this is as a topping for *Swedish Meatballs* (page 182)—unbelievably delicious *and* nutritious!

LIVER GRAVY

1. Chop the liver into ½ x 2-inch slices. Then, dredge the liver in the tapioca flour seasoned with the salt and black pepper.

2. In a large skillet over medium-high heat, add a tablespoon of Lard, and sear the liver (keep it pink on the inside) on both sides, about 2-3 minutes each side. Remove the liver from the pan, and set it aside.

3. Over medium heat, deglaze the brown bits from the pan by slowly adding the Pork Stock as you scrape gently.

4. Add the coconut milk and the browned liver to the skillet. Cook to combine, about 5 minutes.

5. Transfer the liver and Pork Stock to a blender or food processor, and blend until the gravy is thick and smooth. Remember, this is a warm liquid, so be careful while blending!

6. Return the smooth gravy to the skillet, and finish cooking it over medium-low heat until it has thickened to the desired consistency, about 10-15 minutes.

Making this creamy sausage gravy to go on our *Homestyle Biscuits* (page 218) reminds us of the large Southern-style breakfasts that are a Sunday morning staple in our neck of the woods. For a fun and unexpected twist, serve this with *Turnip & Parsnip Purée* (page 224) or *Maple Sage Roasted Butternut Squash* (page 210).

DIFFICULTY
Intermediate

TIME TO TABLE
Less than 30 minutes

SERVES
4-6

INGREDIENTS

1 tablespoon Lard (page 62) or bacon grease

1 pound Maple Sage Breakfast Sausage (page 78), loose

½ cup mushrooms, ¼-inch dice

¼ cup arrowroot powder

2 cups unsweetened almond or light coconut milk (1:3 ratio of water to full-fat coconut milk)

SAUSAGE & MUSHROOM GRAVY

1. Melt the Lard or grease in a skillet over medium heat.

2. Add the sausage and mushrooms to the skillet, and cook them until the sausage is browned and the mushrooms are softened.

3. Add the arrowroot powder to the skillet, and whisk in to combine and thicken the gravy.

4. Slowly pour in the milk while continuously stirring until the gravy is thinned enough to slowly drip off of the spoon. The gravy will thicken again as it continues to cook or sits at room temperature, so serve immediately.

Note: **If your gravy becomes too thick, simply warm over low heat and whisk in additional coconut milk or some Pork Stock until it reaches the desired consistency.**

DIFFICULTY
Intermediate

TIME to TABLE
Less than 30 minutes

YIELD
Makes about ¾ cup

INGREDIENTS

2 egg yolks

1 tablespoon lemon juice

1 teaspoon brown mustard

1 teaspoon salt

¼ teaspoon white pepper

¼ cup bacon fat, melted

¼ cup olive, avocado, or
  macadamia nut oil

Note: Although the acid of the lemon juice will break down the egg proteins to help protect against spoilage, we don't include the preservatives of store-bought mayo, so this recipe only lasts a week, and it needs to be refrigerated.

Our most beloved condiment is mayonnaise. Its *creamy, tangy taste* seems to go with everything. But we wanted to add a salty kick, and what better way to do that than by adding bacon? The resulting Baconnaise (bacon mayonnaise) is simply divine! Make it with fresh herbs to serve with crudité or as the base of our *Spicy Horseradish Pepper Mayonnaise* (page 258).

BACONNAISE

1. In a bowl, beat the egg yolks until they begin to lighten.

2. Add the lemon juice, mustard, salt, and white pepper, and beat for another minute.

3. In a spouted measuring cup, stir together the bacon fat and oil.

4. Very slowly beat the oils into the bowl mixture until a thick sauce forms. At first, drip the oils in slowly. As they become more incorporated into the yolk mixture, pour in a very thin stream until you reach your desired thickness. At the point at which you are able to pour the oil in a thicker stream, a blender or electric mixer can be used. Just be sure not to over-beat the mayonnaise, as it may separate and become irrecoverable.

5. The result will be thinner than store-bought mayonnaise, but it will thicken with refrigeration. You can attempt to make it thicker by beating in more bacon fat if you wish. Chill and only keep for a few days.

DIFFICULTY
Basic

TIME TO TABLE
Less than 30 minutes

YIELD
Makes about ½ cup

EQUIPMENT
Food processor or blender

INGREDIENTS

1 dried chili de arbol (red chili)

½ cup Baconnaise (page 256)

2 tablespoons prepared horseradish, drained

We've talked about the delicious Peruvian rotisserie chicken we eat on the nights we don't cook. While the kids enjoy plain mayonnaise with their chicken, we prefer this *spicy version* that gives it a little kick. The spiciness also works beautifully with the neutral crispiness of *fried Yuca* (page 200), which we generally serve with rotisserie chicken. It's equally yummy on sliced roast beef or as a dip for sweet pepper slices and carrots.

SPICY HORSERADISH PEPPER MAYONNAISE

1. Microwave the chilies, or run them under hot water inside a sealed plastic bag for 20 seconds to soften them.

2. Cut open each chili, and remove the seeds and stems. Then, roughly chop them. Remember to wash your hands after touching the hot peppers, as the oils can irritate your skin and eyes!

3. With a blender or food processor, blend together the chilies with the Baconnaise and horseradish until all ingredients are combined, and the pepper is reduced to tiny specks within the sauce.

4. We recommend that you make this fresh when you are ready to use it since the base is a raw egg yolk mayonnaise. Store chilled for up to a few days.

No cookbook would be complete without a dessert section, even if the subject of that book is pork. The first must-have recipe we planned to include was a classic lard pie crust, but we will prove to even the greatest skeptics that you can go a lot further with pork. If you don't believe us, you haven't tried our Peach and Prosciutto Ice Cream!

That said, a word of caution: some of these treats are super rich. In fact, we've never created a denser, calories-per-square-inch-packed recipe than our Triple Chocolate Freezer Fudge! But that's why they're called treats, right? Save them for special occasions, not nightly binges.

SWEET THANGS

These pancakes are *a great way* to welcome a crisp fall Sunday morning. We roast our own fresh pumpkin, but pure, organic pumpkin purée from a can works just fine, too. If you like, make yourself a batch on the weekend and eat them all week long. According to our boys, the *bite-sized discs* are perfect for on-the-go snacking. For a special occasion, serve them with our *Maple Sage Breakfast Sausage Links* (page 78).

DIFFICULTY
Basic

TIME TABLE
Under 30 minutes

SERVES
4-6

EQUIPMENT
Cast iron skillet recommended; food processor

INGREDIENTS

½ pound Bacon (page 62) (a small handful reserved)

1½ cups pumpkin purée

¼ cup applesauce

¼ cup almond or sunflower seed butter

3 tablespoon maple syrup

6 eggs

¼ teaspoon salt

¼ cup + 2 tablespoon coconut flour

Note: **You can also use store-bought, organic pumpkin purée. Since the water content will vary, additional coconut milk (up to 3 tablespoons) will help the batter come together nicely. The pancakes may also require a longer cooking time, so just pay attention to what's going on in the pan.**

BACON PUMPKIN PANCAKES

1. Fry bacon pieces over medium heat until crispy, about 8 minutes. Set aside on a towel-lined plate or rack to allow grease to drip off and bacon to continue to crisp up as it air dries. Once crispy, crumble or cut into small pieces.

2. Meanwhile, whisk together pumpkin, applesauce, almond butter, eggs and syrup until combined.

3. Add coconut flour and stir until fully incorporated.

4. Using the bacon fat already inside the pan over medium heat, spoon a heaping tablespoon of batter into the pan, then sprinkle with the diced bacon.

5. Let cook for 3-5 minutes per side. Wait patiently, as the pumpkin can have a lot of moisture that needs to cook out. Watch for the bottom of the pancake to darken and become stiff before you attempt to flip.

6. Fry up mini-sized pancakes in small batches until cooked. Store the first batches in a 200°F oven on an oven-safe plate while you cook of the remaining pancakes. Serve with a sprinkle of the remaining bacon and apple butter or 100% pure maple syrup.

DIFFICULTY
Intermediate

TIME to TABLE
30-60 minutes

YIELD
Makes about a pint

INGREDIENTS

5 Bacon slices (page 68), about ½ pound

1 cup full-fat coconut milk

½ cup granulated maple or palm sugar

2 teaspoons baking soda

Note: If you don't want a chunky bacon caramel, purée it once it's finished. If you prefer a less overwhelming bacon taste, don't return the bacon to the pan until the end.

If you would happily pour salted caramel on everything you eat, we get it. How can you not love that *sinfully delicious* combination of salty, sweet, and buttery? Since it's one of Stacy's favorite flavors, we needed to create a version that was slightly less detrimental in the nutrition department, as in no refined sugar or dairy. Enter bacon! We think you'll find our Salted Caramel Bacon Sauce to be the perfect topping for *Maple Pecan Lard Scones* (page 276), a brownie sundae with our *Best Brownies* (page 284), or *Maple Bacon Frozen Custard* (page 282).

SALTED CARAMEL BACON SAUCE

1. In a large skillet over medium heat, fry the bacon until crispy, about 8 minutes. Remove it from the pan, and set it aside on a towel-lined plate or rack to allow it to crisp further as it air dries. Once crispy, crumble or cut the bacon into small pieces.

2. To infuse the sauce with the bacon flavor, dice the bacon and return it to the cooled skillet that still contains the bacon grease. Add the coconut milk, and let the skillet stand for 30 minutes off the heat.

3. Turn the burner to medium heat, and add the granulated sugar to the skillet. Whisk until dissolved.

4. Continue to whisk until the liquid begins to boil, about 10 minutes. When working with coconut milk directly over heat, be careful not to scald it or burn it on the bottom, as this will add a burned flavor to the sauce. The sauce will still be a liquid at this point.

5. Remove the skillet from the heat, and add the baking soda, whisking briskly. The caramel will bubble significantly at first and then subside. If it appears to be ready to overflow, whisk faster to disperse the bubbles. The sauce will continue to thicken as you whisk it off of the heat for 5 minutes.

6. If after sitting out, your sauce "breaks" with the oil rising to the top, simply scoop off most of the top layer of oil, and stir to combine. The sauce should easily recover and be able to be chilled for weeks. Just warm it and stir to combine before serving.

The siren's call of fudge every time you stroll past a candy shop is nearly irresistible. This is one of Stacy's *all-time favorite desserts*, and we squabbled over whether fudge could be made in our kitchen without losing its essential fudginess. Well, you're in luck because Stacy proved that melt-in-your-mouth caramel fudge is not only possible without dairy, *it's superb!*

DIFFICULTY
Advanced

TIME TO TABLE
1-2 hours

YIELD
More than a dozen pieces

EQUIPMENT
Candy thermometer; heavy-bottomed pot

INGREDIENTS

1½ cups maple syrup

1½ cups granulated maple sugar

⅔ cup coconut milk cream (scoop from the top of a cold can of full-fat coconut milk)

1 teaspoon salt

¼ cup Lard (page 62)

1 teaspoon pure vanilla extract

½ cup pecans, chopped

CARAMEL PRALINE LARD FUDGE

1. In a large, heavy-bottomed pot over medium heat, whisk together the maple syrup, granulated sugar, coconut cream, and salt until the sugar dissolves completely.

2. Clip a candy thermometer to the side of the pan so as to monitor the temperature of the mixture.

3. As the syrup cooks, it will start to bubble furiously at about 212°F. Stir and watch it carefully to avoid overflow. If it starts to boil over, whisk the mixture to help the bubbles dissipate.

4. Stir occasionally for about 10 minutes until the temperature of the solution reaches 238°F. When it reaches this temperature, it will be at the soft ball stage.

5. Remove the pan from the heat immediately, and whisk in the Lard and vanilla extract until combined. Fold in the pecans.

6. Pour the fudge into a parchment paper-lined baking dish. We recommend a 9 x 9-inch dish for a greater quantity of cubes or a loaf pan for larger slices. Smooth the top with a spatula, and place the dish in the refrigerator uncovered.

7. Chill for about 1 hour before removing. Do not leave the fudge to chill longer than this, or it will absorb too much moisture. This will make the consistency no longer fudge-like.

8. Remove the parchment paper from the dish, and cut the fudge into 1½-inch cubes or ½-inch thick slices. Store at room temperature. Refrigerating will cause your fudge to crystallize and become gritty.

Some desserts are rich and dense enough that you need just a *single bite to satisfy your sweet tooth*. That would be this Triple Chocolate Freezer Fudge—so decadent and delicious one small serving will satisfy you! Beware, too much of this incredibly rich and dense dessert could be more than your body is willing to handle!

DIFFICULTY
Intermediate

TIME TABLE
30-60 minutes

YIELD
More than a dozen pieces

EQUIPMENT
Double boiler

INGREDIENTS

1½ cups dark chocolate, divided (we recommend mini-chips or finely diced pieces of your favorite bar)

1 cup Lard (page 62), softened

2 tablespoons cocoa powder

1 tablespoon palm or maple granulated sugar

Note: If you don't have a double boiler, you can create the same effect by placing a metal or ceramic bowl over a pan of simmering water; that's simmering, not boiling, and the bowl should *not* touch the water. The steam produced by the simmering water trapped under the bowl allows the chocolate to melt at the proper low temperature, preventing it from burning or sticking to the pan.

TRIPLE CHOCOLATE FREEZER FUDGE

1. Over a double boiler, stirring often, melt 1¼ cups of the chocolate chips.

2. Whisk in the Lard, cocoa, and sugar until thoroughly combined. Then remove the double boiler from the heat.

3. Line a 9 x 9-inch baking dish with parchment paper, and line the bottom with the remaining ¼ cup of chocolate chips.

4. Pour the fudge over the top of the chocolate chips, and smooth it with a spatula.

5. Place the dish in the freezer, and allow the fudge to chill for 1 hour.

6. Remove the fudge from the dish by the parchment paper, and cut it into 1½-inch cubes.

7. An excellent make-ahead dessert, this fudge should be served still cold. Keep it in the freezer until about 10 minutes before serving. The "black bottom" chocolate chips give an excellent texture contrast to this smooth and incredibly rich fudge filling.

One of the greatest innovations in dessert was the discovery that dough balls could be fried into tasty treats. Whether its fritters, doughnuts, or churros, it's clear that people the world over love fried dough! And that includes us. These Apple Fritters are an *incredibly decadent* way to indulge without the grains and oxidized oils found in most fried foods. This recipe makes a large batch perfect *for a party or family event,* especially when paired with our *Maple Bacon Frozen Custard* (page 282).

APPLE FRITTERS

DIFFICULTY
Advanced

TIME to TABLE
Under 30 minutes

SERVES
Up to 10

PREHEAT
Lard in frying pan to 350°F

EQUIPMENT
Electric fryer or heavy-bottomed pot for frying; candy thermometer; food processor

INGREDIENTS

⅔ cup fresh Medjool dates, pits removed (about 10-12)

⅓ cup Lard (page 62), plus additional Lard for frying

2 tablespoons honey

1 tablespoon pure vanilla extract

2½ cups blanched almond flour, divided

1 cup tapioca flour

3 tablespoons arrowroot powder

1 teaspoon cinnamon

1 teaspoon baking soda

¼ teaspoon cream of tartar

¼ teaspoon salt

3 egg whites

2 cups apples, skin removed, finely diced (about 2 medium apples), honeycrisp or pink lady preferred

2 tablespoons granulated maple or palm sugar

1. Purée the dates, Lard, honey, and vanilla together until combined in the food processor.

2. In a separate bowl, sift 1½ cups of the almond flour with the tapioca flour, arrowroot powder, cinnamon, baking soda, cream of tartar, and salt.

3. Add the flour mixture to the wet ingredients, and pulse together until the batter is thick and combined. Set it aside.

4. In a separate bowl, whip the egg whites to soft peaks (so that the egg whites stick to a whisk and form a peak when pulled out without dripping).

5. Gently fold the egg whites, along with the diced apples, into the batter until they are incorporated.

6. Gently mix in the remaining 1 cup of almond flour, ¼ cup at a time, until very sticky dough forms.

7. In an electric fryer or heavy-bottomed pot, heat Lard to 350°F. Drop rounded tablespoons of the dough into the Lard, and fry for about 4 minutes until golden brown and cooked through. (See instructions on frying on page 56.) The oil must be deep enough to completely cover the fritters, or they must be flipped when golden brown and crispy.

8. Once each side of the fritters are golden brown and crispy, remove them from the pan, and place them onto a towel-lined plate or cooling rack to drain and dry.

9. Dust the fritters with a sprinkle of maple sugar.

10. Keep the fritters warm in a 250°F oven as the remaining batches are cooked. They are best eaten fresh out of the fryer, but they also reheat well in the oven or toaster oven.

DIFFICULTY
Intermediate

TIME TO TABLE
30-60 minutes

YIELD
Makes 1 single-layer pie crust

PREHEAT
Oven to 400°F

EQUIPMENT
Electric mixer

INGREDIENTS

½ cup blanched almond flour

½ cup coconut flour

¼ cup tapioca flour

½ cup very cold Lard (page 62) placed in freezer for 10 minutes

½ teaspoon salt

3 tablespoons cold water

Note: **This recipe is savory, which works well with everything in** Beyond Bacon. **If you'd like it sweeter, however, we recommend adding just one tablespoon of honey; don't add more or you risk losing the proper consistency of the dough.**

No doubt, your grandmother made pie crust with lard, and, really, that remains the only way to go. Lard began to fall out of fashion back in 1911, when the vegetable oil Crisco (also called shortening) was introduced. Crisco intended to make the lives of housewives easier, but all it really did was ruin our health by introducing hydrogenated oils into our diet. Often the old ways are the best ways, so the next time your grandmother comes to dinner, whip up this pie crust and remind her that she really did know best. This is also the very first grain-free crust we've ever made that rolls and transfers like the real thing! It's an excellent base for our *Cucumber Dill Quiche* (page 154) or *Dutch Apple Pie* (page 274).

LARD PIE CRUST

1. In a mixing bowl with a hand mixer or in a stand mixer, slowly mix together the almond flour, coconut flour, and tapioca flour.

2. Using ½-inch cubes of the very cold Lard, cut the Lard into the flours with a fork or pastry cutter. Continue to do this until a crumbly mixture forms.

3. Add the salt. Then, add the cold water one tablespoon at a time, using a fork or pastry cutter to incorporate each one.

4. Form the dough into a disk by hand, and wrap it in plastic wrap. Refrigerate it for 30 minutes or until you are ready to roll it out.

5. On top of a wide layer of plastic wrap, roll out the dough into a 10-12-inch circle, about ⅛-inch thick. As there is no gluten or eggs as binding proteins in this crust recipe, the dough will still be slightly crumbly. Handle it carefully. If areas begin to crack, simply bind them back together by pinching the dough with your fingers and lightly rolling it out where the indentation has formed.

6. When ready, turn the 9-inch pie pan upside down on top of the center of the crust. Wrap the edges of the plastic wrap around the backside of the pie pan, and gently flip the crust and pan over. The crust will easily fall into place, but some cracks might need to be fixed as noted in step 5.

7. Remove the plastic wrap, and crimp the edges of the crust with a fork. Dock the crust by poking holes in the bottom with a fork.

8. To prebake the crust, bake for 10 minutes in a 400°F oven.

The Dutch apple pie that inspires this elegant dessert is a testament to simplicity. The topping, made with lardons and lightly spiced, adds a surprising and scrumptious porky accent to the baked apples. It looks very similar to the frozen box pies our family grew up eating, but this is infinitely better. Yet another "I can't believe it's got piggy" classic, especially when served with some *Maple Bacon Frozen Custard* (page 282).

DIFFICULTY
Intermediate

TIME to TABLE
30-60 minutes

SERVES
About 8

PREHEAT
Oven to 350°F

INGREDIENTS
1 Lard Pie Crust (page 272), unbaked

FILLING
5 tart apples, peeled, cored, and thinly sliced

2 tablespoons maple syrup

2 tablespoons tapioca flour

1 tablespoon lemon juice

2 teaspoons cinnamon

1 teaspoon grated nutmeg

½ teaspoon ground allspice

¼ teaspoon ground ginger

TOPPING
¼ cup Crispy Lardons (page 190)

2 tablespoons blanched almond flour

1 tablespoon maple, date, or palm granulated sugar

1 teaspoon cinnamon

¼ cup walnuts, finely chopped

DUTCH APPLE PIE

1. In a large mixing bowl, combine the apples, maple syrup, tapioca flour, and lemon juice with the 2 teaspoons of cinnamon, nutmeg, allspice, and ginger by hand. Let the mixture sit for 10 minutes, then drain the liquid from the bowl.

2. Layer the apples in the prebaked pie crust, making sure there are no large gaps.

3. In a small bowl, combine the Crispy Lardons, almond flour, granulated sugar, cinnamon, and walnuts into a crumbly mixture to create the topping.

4. Sprinkle the Lardon mixture over the apples, being careful to evenly cover the top of the pie.

5. Bake the pie at 350°F for 45 minutes.

6. Let it sit for 20-30 minutes before slicing. Store chilled, and reheat it in the oven.

DIFFICULTY
Basic

TIME to TABLE
Under 30 minutes

YIELD
Makes 8 large scones or 24 small scones

PREHEAT
Oven to 325°F

EQUIPMENT
Electric mixer

INGREDIENTS

¼ cup Lard (page 62), cold

2 cups blanched almond flour

¼ cup granulated maple sugar

1 teaspoon baking soda

½ teaspoon cream of tartar

½ teaspoon salt

1 egg

2 tablespoons full-fat coconut milk

1 teaspoon pure vanilla extract

½ cup chopped pecans (optional)

Tapioca flour for dusting, a few tablespoons

Note: **If you want to kick it up a notch, drizzle the baked scones with Salted Caramel Bacon Sauce (page 264) and toasted pecans.**

Tea scones were not on our *Beyond Bacon* must list at first. But we had such fantastic luck perfecting the *Salted Mocha Biscotti* (page 292), we thought we'd give it a shot. And thank goodness; we were thrilled with the results! Where traditional scones are often dry and tasteless, these are light and flavorful. They will make a *beautiful presentation* at your next tea party or potluck.

MAPLE PECAN LARD SCONES

1. With an electric mixer, whip the Lard until fluffy.

2. Sift together the almond flour, granulated sugar, baking soda, cream of tartar, and salt until thoroughly incorporated. Then, using the electric mixer, mix the dry ingredients on low with the Lard until combined.

3. Add the egg, coconut milk, and vanilla extract, and continue to beat until thick dough forms.

4. Fold in the chopped pecans with a spatula. The dough should be firm and flexible. If your dough is too wet to manipulate, refrigerate it for 30 minutes to allow it to firm up.

5. Turn the dough out onto a very lightly-floured surface, and roll it into a 12-inch diameter and ½-inch tall circular disk. Try to handle it as little as possible, as the lighter you roll, the less dense and dry your scones will turn out. Be sure to make your disk as even and circular as possible so that your wedges will be able to be sized evenly for consistent baking.

6. Cut the dough into 8 equal wedges. If serving a crowd, cut each scone into thirds (for 24 small scones). Spread the wedges apart on a baking sheet. They puff but do not spread, so they can bake relatively close together.

7. Bake at 325°F for 18-20 minutes.

This dish is pretty ubiquitous at this point; why offer up another recipe? Because those who haven't experienced this literal *meat candy* really need to do so! We haven't messed with what is already a perfect recipe: the combination of crispy-soft-crunchy-sweet-salty simply can't be improved upon! These bite-sized treats are a great in-a-pinch appetizer, or as a quick, on-the-run snack. Our kids and adult friends beg for them!

DIFFICULTY
Basic

TIME TABLE
Under 30 minutes

YIELD
Makes about 30

PREHEAT
425°F

EQUIPMENT
Wire cooling rack

INGREDIENTS
1 pound fresh Medjool dates (about 30)

¼ cup almonds, blanched and skin removed recommended (optional)

1 pound Bacon (page 68)

BACON WRAPPED DATES

1. Create the baking set-up by inserting the elevated wire cooling rack into a baking sheet. This will allow the bacon to crisp on all sides as you cook the date rolls.

2. Slice through one side of each date enough to open it in half and remove the pit. Do not cut them fully in half, however, as they need to be intact to encase the nuts. The dates should be soft and pliable; if they are stiff to the touch, they have already been dried and will become tough when baked.

3. Place a nut inside each date where the pit was, and close the date. Be careful to keep the piles separate, as the almonds and date pits look nearly identical. You don't want to accidentally replace the pits into the dates!

4. Cut the bacon strips into halves or thirds, depending on the size of the dates, and wrap each date with bacon. Place them on the wire rack with the loose end of the bacon on the underside so that it doesn't unroll as they cook.

5. Bake for 8 minutes at 425°F until the bacon is crispy.

Note: **We played with the stuffing of this recipe and decided the original was still our favorite. But if you want to give your favorite nut a chance, pecans, walnuts, and pistachios all work well. If you eat dairy, you can also fill the dates with a soft cheese, then wrap in prosciutto for an amazing addition to a salami tray!**

You're probably wondering if watching *Iron Chef* inspired this crazy concoction; that show is the only other place you'd think to see *pork combined with ice cream*. But we imagine it's pretty clear by now that we love the combination of salty and sweet, and this recipe fills the bill spectacularly. The creamy coconut milk is a perfect compliment to *the sweet summer flavor* of a ripe roasted peach, and when you add the subtle, salted, buttery flavor of prosciutto? Wow! Serve it to guests and we guarantee you'll talk of nothing else for the rest of the evening.

PROSCIUTTO AND ROASTED PEACH ICE CREAM

DIFFICULTY
Intermediate

TIME TO TABLE
3-6 hours

SERVES
6-8

PREP
Oven to 350°F; freeze ice cream maker bowl overnight

EQUIPMENT
Ice cream maker; blender or food processor

INGREDIENTS

4 ripe peaches

1 tablespoon gelatin, grass-fed recommended

¼ cup boiling water

8 thick slices high quality prosciutto, about 2-3 ounces, diced

13.5-ounce can full-fat coconut milk

2 cups unsweetened almond milk

⅓ cup honey, raw recommended

1½ teaspoons pure vanilla extract

1. Cut the peaches in half, and remove the pits. Cut a shallow "X" in the rounded edge of the skin of each peach half (this will help with skin removal after cooking), and place them, flat side down, on the baking sheet.

2. Roast (or grill) the peach halves for 30 minutes at 350°F. After roasting, allow the peaches to cool for 5-10 minutes until they are cool enough to handle. Do not cool too long, or the skins will be difficult to remove. Once slightly cooled, remove the skin of each peach, and dice them into bite-sized pieces.

3. While waiting for the peaches to cool, dissolve the gelatin in the boiling water, and dice the prosciutto into very small bite-sized pieces. The larger the piece, the more of a flavor it will impart as the ice cream is eaten (¼-½-inch squares are recommended).

4. Add half of the diced peaches, coconut milk, almond milk, honey, and vanilla extract to the blender, and purée until smooth.

5. Add gelatin to the mixture, and blend again for 1 minute.

6. Place the ice cream mixture into the refrigerator for 1 hour to chill.

7. Set aside the remaining diced peaches and diced prosciutto.

8. Churn the chilled mixture in an ice cream maker for 10-20 minutes until it is thick and creamy.

9. Add the prosciutto and the rest of the peaches to the ice cream maker, and churn for another 2-3 minutes to fully incorporate.

10. Remove the ice cream from the bowl, and transfer it into a storage container for the freezer. Freeze for 2-4 hours before serving. Longer storage will harden the ice cream.

Note: The gelatin in this recipe not only assists in creating a soft texture similar to store-bought ice cream, it adds healthy collagen. However, since there are no chemical additives, it will harden to a solid state if frozen for more than the recommended hours. To thaw, simply set it out at room temperature for 20-30 minutes before serving. Texture is best when served the same day it was made!

DIFFICULTY
Intermediate

TIME to TABLE
Less than 3 hours

SERVES
6-8

PREP
Freeze ice cream maker bowl overnight

EQUIPMENT
Ice cream maker; blender or food processor

INGREDIENTS

1 tablespoon gelatin, grass-fed recommended

¼ cups boiling water

13.5-ounce can full-fat coconut milk

2 cups unsweetened almond milk

½ cup maple syrup, grade B recommended

4 large egg yolks

1 tablespoon pure vanilla extract

1 teaspoon hazelnut or almond extract (optional)

4-6 pieces Bacon (page 68), crispy and diced into small pieces

½ cup fresh or dried Medjool dates, diced very small (optional)

½ cup dark chocolate chips (optional)

Frozen custard, a Midwest favorite, is the richer and creamier cousin of ice cream. We find that we prefer the taste and texture of custard in our frozen treats. Since the recipe calls for raw egg yolks, we recommend only using *pastured eggs*; they are less likely to contain the harmful bacteria found in the non-pastured variety. We originally thought of this recipe after visiting Sally Fallon Morell at her P.A. Bowen Farmstead. The eggs we purchased contained the healthiest and deepest orange yolks we'd ever seen, and this recipe takes advantage of their *naturally rich and creamy sweetness.*

MAPLE BACON FROZEN CUSTARD

1. Dissolve the gelatin in the boiling water.

2. Add the coconut milk, almond milk, maple syrup, egg yolks, vanilla extract, and hazelnut or almond extract to the blender or food processor, and purée the mixture until smooth.

3. Add the gelatin to the blender, and blend again for 1 minute.

4. Place the ice cream mixture in the refrigerator for 1 hour to chill.

5. Churn the chilled mixture in an ice cream maker for 10-20 minutes until it is thick and creamy.

6. Add the diced bacon and dates and/or chocolate chips, and churn for another 2-3 minutes to fully incorporate the ingredients.

7. Remove the ice cream from the bowl, and transfer it into a storage container for the freezer. Freeze for 2-4 hours before serving.

8. If frozen for longer, the texture will become frozen solid. To thaw, simply set it out at room temperature for 20-30 minutes before you're ready to serve it. The texture is best the same day it is made!

Note: For those worried about foodborne pathogens, yes, it is possible to cook this custard to eliminate any potential risks for illness. Simply pour the milks and syrups into a pot and cook over medium heat until it just begins to bubble. Whisk your egg yolks together and then temper the yolks by adding small portions of the milk mixture and whisking, until about ⅓ of the milk is with the yolks. Pour the warmed yolks into the remainder of the milk mixture and continue to simmer for another ten minutes before adding the dissolved gelatin and vanilla and whisking together. Place this mixture in the fridge and chill for one hour, then churn as normal.

These brownies are a classic favorite on our website and for good reason: they are perfectly dense and chewy, with a rich and deep *chocolate flavor*. There's not much more to say, other than that they are the best brownies we've had!

For the ultimate treat, top with any combination of *Prosciutto and Roasted Peach Ice Cream* (page 280), *Maple Bacon Frozen Custard* (page 282), *Crispy Lardons* (page 190), and *Salted Caramel Bacon Sauce* (page 264).

DIFFICULTY
Basic

TIME to TABLE
30-60 minutes

SERVES
8-10

PREHEAT
Oven to 350°F

EQUIPMENT
Electric mixer

INGREDIENTS

½ cup maple syrup, Grade B preferred

⅓ cup Lard (page 62), room temperature

2 large eggs

2½ cups blanched almond flour

¼ cup cocoa powder

1 teaspoon baking soda

½ teaspoon salt

½ cup dark chocolate chips

½ cup raw macadamia nuts, chopped (optional)

THE BEST BROWNIES

1. In a medium bowl, using an electric mixer, whisk together the maple syrup and Lard.

2. Add the eggs one at a time, and beat the mixture together.

3. In a separate bowl, sift together the almond flour, cocoa, baking soda, and salt.

4. Add the dry ingredients to the egg mixture, and mix together until a batter forms.

5. Fold in the chocolate chips and nuts with a spatula.

6. Pour the batter into an 8 x 8-inch baking dish that has been greased with Lard.

7. Bake the brownies at 350°F for about 25 minutes or until the center is almost firm and the top is slightly browned. Let the brownies sit in the dish at room temperature for at least 20-30 minutes to allow the melted chocolate to cool. The temptation to sneak a piece will be difficult to resist, but the texture will be much better with patience!

Note: For parties or events, we recommend doubling this recipe and cooking it in a 13 x 9-inch pan for an additional 5-10 minutes, until the center is almost firm.

Growing up, Matt thought that all cake came from a mix in a box; the idea of his baking a cake without one seemed impossible. Now he makes all our cakes from scratch and it's surprisingly easy. This version of a traditional yellow cake is our go-to recipe for birthdays. It's made with nutrient-dense pastured egg yolks and is completely nut-free! We recommend frosting it with our *Chocolate "Butter" Cream Frosting* (page 288).

YELLOW LARD CAKE

DIFFICULTY
Intermediate

TIME TO TABLE
Under 30 minutes

YIELD
1 dozen cupcakes

PREHEAT
Oven to 350°F

EQUIPMENT
Electric mixer

INGREDIENTS

½ cup Lard (page 62), room temperature

½ cup honey

1½ teaspoons pure vanilla extract

3 eggs plus 2 egg yolks

¾ cup coconut flour

½ teaspoon baking soda

½ teaspoon salt

Note: We often choose to make cupcakes to avoid excess cake spoiling on the counter. You can make them in smaller batches or they can freeze easily. If you wish to make a layer cake for a special occasion, double the recipe and line two greased 9-inch round cake pans with parchment paper. Bake for 21-23 minutes, or until the tops are golden brown. Let them cool completely before stacking. Fill the layers with fresh berries mixed with jam.

1. Using an electric mixer, beat the Lard and honey together on high for 3 minutes until they are light and fluffy.

2. Add the vanilla extract, eggs, and egg yolks, and whip until fully incorporated with the Lard and honey.

3. Measure the coconut flour by scooping it loosely and using a knife or flat utensil to scrape off the top edge for an even measurement.

4. In a separate bowl, sift together the coconut flour, baking soda, and salt.

5. Slowly beat the flour mixture into the wet ingredients on medium-low until smooth.

6. Fill muffin liners (silicone or aluminum foil recommended) in a muffin tin ⅔ of the way full with the batter (these cupcakes do not rise much). For pretty tops, smooth the tops of the cupcakes with the back of a spoon or spreading knife dipped in oil.

7. Bake for 16-18 minutes at 350°F or until the tops of the cupcakes are golden brown and a toothpick inserted in the middle comes out clean.

8. Allow the cupcakes to cool completely before icing.

DIFFICULTY
Basic

TIME to TABLE
30-60 minutes

YIELD
Frosts 24 cupcakes or one
9-inch layer cake

EQUIPMENT
Food processor or electric
mixer

INGREDIENTS

⅓ cup dark chocolate chips
or grated chocolate bar

2 cups Lard (page 62), cold

⅓ cup granulated maple,
date, or palm sugar

2 tablespoons cocoa powder

1 teaspoon pure vanilla
extract

2 tablespoons full-fat
coconut milk

We used to love eating cupcakes. But since eliminating diary, our family just can't eat buttercream frosting anymore. We enjoy the challenge of *recreating old favorites*, so we jumped right into creating this buttery frosting that includes no butter (or dairy) at all! This is one of those recipes that surprised even us what lard can do!

CHOCOLATE "BUTTER" CREAM FROSTING

1. Using a food processor or electric mixer, chop the chocolate chips into a fine grain-like texture. The end product will still have small chocolate pieces but be small enough to melt easily on the tongue. If using a chocolate bar, a grater is recommended.

2. Add the Lard, sugar, cocoa, vanilla extract, and coconut milk. Purée or whisk until smooth. The frosting at this point will be very thin.

3. Transfer the frosting to a mixing bowl, and cover it with plastic wrap.

4. Refrigerate the frosting for 30 minutes to thicken. When ready to use, spread the frosting on your cooled cake or cupcakes. Refrigerate until ready to serve. Then, allow the cakes or cupcakes to sit for 15 minutes at room temperature before serving.

Note: **Although a great make-ahead dish, please be aware that, like a true buttercream, this frosting will soften and melt if it gets too warm. Be sure to chill until you are ready to serve it!**

DIFFICULTY
Basic

TIME *to* TABLE
Less than 45 minutes

YIELD
Makes 2 dozen muffins

PREHEAT
Oven to 325°F

INGREDIENTS

4 cups blanched almond flour

1 teaspoon baking soda

1 teaspoon salt

1 tablespoon cinnamon

1 teaspoon ground cardamom

½ teaspoon ground cloves

½ teaspoon ground ginger

½ cup Lard (page 62)

¼ cup maple syrup

¼ cup honey

4 eggs

1 tablespoon pure vanilla extract

2 medium apples, grated and strained

1 cup dried cranberries

1¼ cups pistachios, roasted and chopped

For hundreds of years, at the end of autumn, when all the season's harvest was in, it was traditional to make *harvest cakes*. From this we get the original carrot cakes, pumpkin pies, apple pies, and zucchini breads. Our version of a harvest muffin includes not just apples, but cranberries and pistachios. It's a wonderful way to welcome cool autumn mornings.

HARVEST MUFFINS

1. In a bowl, sift together the almond flour, baking soda, salt, cinnamon, cardamom, cloves, and ginger.

2. In a separate bowl, beat the Lard, maple syrup, honey, eggs, and vanilla extract until well combined

3. Add the dry ingredients and the apples to the wet ingredients and mix well until fully incorporated.

4. Fold in the cranberries and pistachios with a rubber spatula.

5. Spoon ¼ cup of the batter into muffin cups lined with silicone or aluminum foil liners, about ⅔ full.

6. Bake the muffins for 30 minutes or until a toothpick inserted into the center comes out clean.

7. Cool the muffins for 10 minutes. Then, remove each muffin from the muffin tin.

8. The muffins will keep up to several days at room temperature and can be frozen for months.

DIFFICULTY
Intermediate

TIME to TABLE
1-2 hours

YIELD
About 2 dozen biscotti

PREHEAT
Oven to 350°F

EQUIPMENT
Electric mixer

INGREDIENTS

2½ cups blanched almond flour

½ cup cocoa powder

½ cup arrowroot powder

1½ tablespoons ground coffee

½ teaspoon kosher salt

1 teaspoon baking soda

¼ cup Lard (page 62), room temperature

1 egg

¼ cup maple syrup

¼ cup fresh Medjool dates, pit removed and chopped

¾ cup dark chocolate chips

Stacy's mother is a biscotti connoisseur. Well, she was until we convinced her to go *grain-free* last year. It took quite a few rounds in our test kitchen to get this one just right, but when we did, the glee on Stacy's mom's face made it time well spent. The texture of these treats is *dense and crisp*, just the way biscotti should be. So go ahead, dunk away in your morning coffee. Who knows, you might not need that sugary mocha coffee fix from your favorite coffee house anymore!

SALTED MOCHA BISCOTTI

1. In a bowl, sift the almond flour, cocoa, arrowroot powder, ground coffee, salt, and baking soda together. Set the mixture aside.

2. In a separate bowl, cream together the Lard, egg, maple syrup, and chopped dates using an electric mixer on medium-high.

3. Slowly add the dry ingredients to the wet ingredients, and mix on a low setting until just combined. Do not over-beat, or the dough consistency will change.

4. Fold in the chocolate chips, and fully combine them in the batter.

5. Form 2 12 x 1-inch logs on a parchment paper-lined baking sheet.

6. Bake the logs at 350°F for 25 minutes.

7. Remove the logs from the oven (do not remove from the baking sheet), and let them cool for at least 1 hour or until the chocolate chips are no longer soft and melty.

8. Slice the cooled logs on the bias to the preferred width of the biscotti. We recommend ¾-1-inch slices. The logs should make about 2 dozen biscotti if you use this size.

9. Once cut, place the biscotti sliced side up (doesn't matter which side) on a baking sheet, and bake them at 300°F for 15 minutes until almost crispy. They will harden slightly after cooling.

10. Serve the biscotti at room temperature with coffee. Store in an airtight container for a few days. Then, chill or freeze the biscotti to keep them fresh longer.

INDEX

RESOURCES

Find Us:

- PaleoParents.com
- Our first cookbook, *Eat Like a Dinosaur* paleoparents.com/eat-like-a-dinosaur/
- Podcast: The Paleo View, paleoparents.com/the-paleo-view-podcast/
- Facebook, Twitter, Instagram, YouTube, and Pinterest: @PaleoParents

On Paleo:

- BalancedBites.com and *Practical Paleo* by Diane Sanfilippo
- ChrisKressser.com by Chris Kresser
- Mark's Daily Apple and *The Primal Blueprint* by Mark Sisson
- RobbWolf.com and *The Paleo Solution* by Robb Wolf
- ThePaleoMom.com and *The Paleo Approach* by Sarah Ballantyne

Meat Sources:

- US Wellness Meats, http://is.gd/uswellnessmeats
- EatWild.com
- Polyface Farms, PolyfaceFarms.com
- Mount Vernon Farm, MountVernonGrassfed.com
- The Organic Butcher of McLean, TheOrganicButcher.com

Ingredients We Use:

- Honeyville Blanched Almond Flour, http://is.gd/HoneyvilleAlmondFlour
- Bob's Red Mill Tapioca Flour, http://is.gd/TapiocaFlour
- Bob's Red Mill Arrowroot Flour (Powder), http://is.gd/Arrowroot
- Tropical Traditions Coconut (flour, oil, flakes), http://is.gd/TTCoconut
- Coconut Secret Coconut Aminos, http://is.gd/CoconutAminos
- Natural Value Coconut Milk (No Additives and BPA-free), http://is.gd/CoconutMilk
- Red Boat Fish Sauce, http://is.gd/RedBoat
- Big Tree Farms Coconut Palm Sugar, http://is.gd/PalmSugar
- Health Best Organic Maple Sugar, http://is.gd/MapleSugar
- Tropical Traditions Maple Syrup (Grade B), http://is.gd/TTMapleSyrup
- Enjoy Life Chocolate Chips, http://is.gd/ChocolateChips
- Maine Coast Sea Salt with Sea Vegetables, http://is.gd/SeaVeg

Tools We Use:

- KitchenAid Mixer, http://is.gd/KitchenAid
- KitchenAid Meat Grinder Attachment, http://is.gd/MeatGrinder
- Cuisinart Food Processor, http://is.gd/FoodProcessor
- Cuisinart Ice Cream Maker, http://is.gd/IceCreamMaker
- Le Creuset Cookware, http://is.gd/LeCreuset
- Staub Cookware, http://is.gd/StaubCook
- Lodge Cookware, http://is.gd/LodgeCook
- Waring Dehydrator (regular) http://is.gd/Dehydrator
- Excalibur Dehydrator (large) http://is.gd/LargeDehydrator
- Paderno World Cuisine Vegetable Noodle Maker, http://is.gd/SpiralSlicer

Art and Photography:

- Aimee Buxton, AimeeBuxtonPhotography.com
- Molly Peterson, MollyMPeterson.com
- CJ Hughes, CustomChalk.com
- Drywell Art, DrywellArt.com

SPECIAL THANKS TO

To our 3 sons: *Cole, Finian and Wesley*—for having the patience to understand that sometimes we could only read one book instead of three before bed because *Beyond Bacon* was waiting. For helping us invent new ideas and always telling the truth when trying out our recipes. And for reminding us how fragile and vulnerable we all are in this world, inspiring us to find personal fortitude and the strength we needed to change our lives to live the happiest, healthiest and fullest lives together we possibly can.

Our *family and friends*, who span across states, countries and continents—many of whom reside most often on the other side of a computer screen, yet their support enveloped and encouraged us to take this leap and trust our instincts and vision. Without the village of love with which we're lucky to have, none of this would be possible. From the sharing of resources and being sounding boards for brainstorming of ideas to playing with our children when we needed time to focus on writing—it is not without these beloved people in our lives that we succeed; for we are only as good as those people who surround us and drive us to be the best versions of ourselves.

To our *readers and fans*, for the positive encouragement and reinforcement that the time we devote to this movement adds value and changes lives for the better. The community around us provides nourishment to our souls and keeps us going strong!

To our publisher, *Erich and Michele at Victory Belt*, for having had not only the original faith in our vision but continuing to foster and encourage our growth, for spending endlessly long hours helping to perfect this book. *Beyond Bacon* would not be the work of art it is without their willingness to choose quality each time a crucial choice needed to be made.

CJ Hughes for taking our crazy chalkboard idea and turning it into an eye-catching book cover.

Molly Peterson for her beautiful photography of happy, pastured pigs.

Mike Peterson for inviting us onto his farm countless times and showing our children not only where their food comes from, but how important it is that it be treated with respect.

Don Roden for being the kind of genuinely helpful and service-minded butcher my grandmother would have been happy to patron.

Joel Salatin for graciously agreeing to write the foreword to this book, sight unseen, and other general awesomeness that contributes to the sustainable farming movement—making this earth a better place for my children's children.

Aimee Buxton for her mouth-watering photography, supportive encouragement to step out of our comfort zone to try new things and being the best partner we could have asked for.

301

REFERENCES

1. Salatin, Joel. "Polyface Guiding Principles". http://www.polyfacefarms.com/principles/.

2. Beck, Simone, Bertholle, Louisette, Child, Julia. Mastering the Art of French Cooking. New York: Alfred A. Knopf, 1961. Print.

3. Crea, Joe. (Tuesday, October 27, 2009). Thought for Food: Michael's Symon's sage advice. Symon, Michael. Clevland.com. Retrieved from: http://blog.cleveland.com/pdextra/2009/10/thought_for_food_michael_symon.html

4. Butler, Kiera. (January 3, 2011). "Two Young, Attractive Ladies Taking Down Some Hogs". Mother Jones. Retrieved from: http://www.motherjones.com/environment/2010/12/naomi-pomeroy-beast-meat

5. Kiple, Kenneth "Hogs" The Cambridge World History of Food Retrieved from: http://www.cambridge.org/us/books/kiple/hogs.htm

6. "Trichinellosis" Centers for Disease Control and Prevention, Retrieved from: http://www.cdc.gov/parasites/trichinellosis/index.html

7. Pollan, Michael. The Omnivore's Dilemma: A Natural History of Four Meals. New York: Penguin, 2006. Print.

8. Fallon, Sally, "Know Your Fats Introduction", WestonAPrice.org, Web, February 24, 2009.

9. Enig, Mary, Fallon, Sally. Nourishing Traditions: The Cookbook that Challenges Politically Correct Nutrition and the Deit Dictocrats. Newtrends Publishing, Inc., 1999. Print.

10. Siri-Tarino, Patty W, Sun, Qi, Hu, Frank and Krauss, Ronald, "Meta-analysis of prospective cohort studies evaluating the association of saturated fat with cardiovascular disease", American Journal of Clinical Nutrition, January 2010

11. Sisson, Mark. The Primal Blueprint: Reprogram your genes for effortless weight loss, vibrant health, and boundless energy. Primal Nutrition, Inc., 2009. Print.

12. Jaminet, Paul "The Trouble with Pork, Part 3: Pathogens", PerfectHealthDiet.com, Web February 22, 2012.

13. Mercola, Joseph, "Why I Do Not Recommend Pork - Nearly 70 Percent Contaminated with Dangerous Pathogens", Mercola.com, Web, December 12, 2012.

14. Rubik, Beverly, "How Does Pork Prepared in Various Ways Affect the Blood?", Wise Traditions in Food, Farming and the Healing Arts, Weston A Price Foundation, Fall 2011.

15. Smith-DeWaal, Caroline, Tian, Xuman Amanda, Bhuiya, Farida, "Outbreak Alert! 2008", Center for Science in the Public Interest, Retrieved from: http://www.cspinet.org/new/pdf/outbreak_alert_2008_report_final.pdf.

16. Bourdain, Anthony. Kitchen Confidential: Adventures in the Culinary Underbelly. New York: Bloomsbury Publishing, 2000. Print.

17. Henderson, Fergus. The Whole Beast: Nose to Tail Eating. New York: HarperCollins, 2004. Print.

18. Jefferson, Thomas. "Thomas Jefferson to Alexander Donald". The Founders' Constitution. Volume 4. Article 7. Document 12. (1788). The University of Chicago Press.

19. Hurd, Rebecca Smith. (June 2004). "The Thermochemical Joy of Cooking". Wired Magazine. Retrieved from: http://www.wired.com/wired/archive/12.06/cooking.html

20. Sanfilippo, Diane. "4 Super-foods the media tells you are unhealthy". BalancedBites.com. Web. March 8, 2013.

21. Kresser, Chris. "5 fats you should be cooking with – but may not be". ChrisKresser.com. Web. February 17, 2011.

CONVERSION TABLE

LIQUIDS

US	Metric
1 teaspoon	5 mL
1 tablespoon or ½ fluid ounce	15 mL
1 fluid ounce or ⅛ cup	30 mL
¼ cup or 2 fluid ounces	60 mL
⅓ cup	80 mL
½ cup or 4 fluid ounces	120 mL
⅔ cup	160 mL
¾ cup or 6 fluid ounces	180 mL
1 cup or 8 fluid ounces	240 mL
1½ cups or 12 fluid ounces	350 mL
2 cups or 16 fluid ounces	475 mL

WEIGHT

US	Metric
1 ounce	28 g
4 ounces or ¼ pound	113 g
⅓ pound	150 g
8 ounces or ½ pound	230 g
⅔ pound	300 g
12 ounces or ¾ pound	340 g

TEMPERATURE

Fahrenheit	Celsius
0°	-18°
32°	0°
180°	82°
212°	100°
250°	120°
350°	175°
425°	220°
500°	260°

LENGTH

US	Metric
⅛ inch	3 mm
¼ inch	6 mm
½ inch	13 mm
¾ inch	19 mm
1 inch	2.5 cm
6 inches	15 cm

Michael Symon

FACTORS for HEART DISEASE."
Mark Sisson

"RICH IN VITAMIN D AND HEAT-STABLE, THIS TRADITIONAL FAT IS A TOP-PICK OF MINE FOR COOKING AND NUTRIENTS..."
Diane Sanfilippo

"DON'T EAT ANYTHING your great grandmother WOULDN'T RECOGNIZE AS FOOD... You may need to go back to your great-or even great-great grandmother."
Michael Pollan

'PORK FAT rules!
Emeril Lagasse

"I got A WHOLE PIG A COUPLE WEEKS AGO. We saved every single part of that animal. Nothing went unused... it's incredible TO USE ALL THE PARTS OF A PIG"
Naomi Pomeroy

To me, ...out VEAL STOCK, ...AT, SAUSAGE, ...AT, DEMI-GLACE, ...STINKY CHEESE ...e not worth ...iving."
...ny Bourdain

I always use my 'Holy Trinity' which is SALT, OLIVE OIL AND BACON. MY MOTTO IS, 'BACON ALWAYS MAKES IT BETTER.' I try to use bacon and pork products whenever I can.
Anne Burrell

...t's only polite ...ly if you knock ...animal on the ...d to eat it all: ...E, HEART, FEET, ...RS, HEAD, TAIL. It's all ...OD STUFF."
...gus Henderson

That is, the diet of the animals we eat has a bearing on the NUTRITIONAL QUALITY, and the healthfulness, of the food itself, whether it is MEAT or MILK or EGGS.
Michael Pollan

"PRAISE THE LARD!"
Stacy Toth

"Go to the grocery store and ...things Buy QUALITY

...cting and honoring